3rd Event Horizon

Shannon D.C.

Creative Cover Art Design by : L. D. Mora

SDC Publishing
1637 Valley Pkwy Ste 217
Escondido, CA 92027

First Edition

Dedication:

This book is dedicated to my Abba Father first,
He who reached down and noticed me
And my earthly father who now worships at His
feet.

Letter to the reader

You're at that point. You've been there many times throughout your life.

The precipice.

It is a word that evokes anxiety, anticipation, fear and excitement; Marriage, the birth of a child, becoming an adult, fighting the good fight, losing someone in death.   All precipices that as we fall we are stretched and molded, learn and grow, or slow, or just don't go.

Here is a precipice.

From this point forward you will know about the Third Event Horizon.

I write this as a layman. I have absolutely no scientific skills, but I believe the Lord provides what we lack and if we will let Him, He will guide and direct us to His purpose.

You have been challenged. Stand on the precipice. Let yourself fall. Whether you grow, slow, or don't go, you may have a glimpse at what will be the formation of the new Heaven and new Earth.

John Beloved

Preface

April 5, 2012 – San Diego, California

He comes. He comes.

John Beloved blinked open sleepless eyes.

The room around him was familiar. The bed he lay in was a marriage bed he'd shared for almost thirty years with his wife Annie. She'd become his other half, his conscience, his rock, and who was apparently already up and moving.

He comes, He comes; a solemn decree, a frightening proposition, a wondrous thought.

These two small words, repeated again and again in his heart for over a month, had swelled and grown until they'd become a mantra that woke him in the morning or eased him to sleep at night.

The words never threatened. Instead, they stirred both an overwhelming sense of joy... no no, not joy, hope and at the same time provoked an overwhelming sense of fear.

Two tiny words clenching at his soul, leaving him shaken. He could only liken it to ascending to the highest point of a rollercoaster and looking out into eternity right before the drop. A heady mixture of excitement and apprehension so profound he couldn't define it with human language.

He heard routine stirring in the house and swung his legs over the edge of the bed. Remaining seated, he waited for his blood to start circulating and his body to catch up to his mind.

He comes, He comes.

What was most amazing about these two words, he thought, what was life-changing about them, was the way they resonated in his body like an alarm clock. A timer if you will, he reflected, that awakened him to truth; a spiritual truth that allowed no equivocation.

John remembered sharing the words with Annie (Annabelle Denney-Beloved if you asked her) from the first moment they'd resounded in his being. It had been late morning, and they'd both been standing in the kitchen sipping coffee when John shared his revelation.

Annie had nodded her head slowly, quietly allowing herself time to process all the words implied. She'd turned away from him and looked out the window to where their daughter Sara stood talking and laughing with friends.

"Yes John." she had replied, her understanding of the gravity and urgency of the words as profound as his own.

"Yes", she'd said again, but he had heard the unspoken question in her voice. Were they prepared? Or more precisely, was Sara?

Shaking off the memory, John stood to dress himself.

"Today we will begin our journey to His glory." John thought reverently as he pulled a t-shirt over his head and stepped into his jeans, hoisting them up with his resolve.

The Holy Spirit moved in him, confirming his decision, and he said "Thank You" in his spirit.

He was aware that in order to begin their battle they must start with their past.

They must consider and acknowledge the path which had led to the message now firmly implanted in his head and his heart.

Back some ten years or so, to the beginning, when he and Annie had taken the children on a road trip…

Chapter 1

June 10, 2001 – Beloved Family Road Trip

Annie inscribed the date and title onto the front of her new journal as John and the children finished packing. She felt the excitement of the trip and the anticipation of adventures yet to unfold.

She loved making memories with her family and documented each trip in its' own journal, a chronology of times and places that touched her heart, stories or jokes her children told, and sentiments she experienced.

Annie felt this was a special trip. She wasn't sure why she felt this way, but she assumed it was connected with her children's ages.

"The kids are growing up.", she thought. "This might be their last family vacation for a while, maybe ever."

Her children Chris and Sara were seventeen and fifteen and she'd felt, just a little and for the first time, their reluctance to give up fourteen days of their summer with their friends.

So Annie decided this year she would be especially focused on capturing all she could just in case. She finished her journal title and gazed out on the front lawn from her vantage point near the sink.

She was quite lost in thought when John stepped into the warm kitchen, brightly lit by the morning sun and found Annie awash in streaks of light.

Unable to stop himself, John assumed his ninja stance. Sliding up to her quietly from behind, he grabbed her midsection with both hands and yelled, "Boo!"

Annie jumped, startled by the playful assault, and turned quickly to face him, laughing and punching at his gut.

"Butt face! I'm getting old John Beloved! Are you trying to give me a heart attack"?

"You're not old babe, your older" he replied with a serious face, but a smile in his voice.

Annie lightly swatted at his head, "you're supposed to say you're not old babe and leave it at that".

John tightened his grasp around Annie's waist pulling her to him.

"You're not old babe" he whispered, his breath warm in her ear, while his hands started to roam down her backside.

"Honey!" Annie giggled, pushing at his lecherous hands, "Stop! We need to get going before the kids decide they want to stay home!"

John, unperturbed, smacked her behind and yelled for his children to "stop messing around and get their gear together" before he kissed his wife's cheek and ambled out the door leading to the garage.

Chris Beloved heard his father yelling as he sat at the computer desk in his room. He was reviewing a comment left by a friend regarding a girl they were both interested in.

Her social media page was like an open book giving Chris fresh insight on how to proceed.

He quickly replies to his friend's barb with a smile reflective of a cat with the canary. Above average in intelligence, he'd already set in motion a plan guaranteeing a victory that would culminate in a date with the lovely Ella. If only he didn't have to go on this ridiculous family vacation.

He was seventeen for crying out loud! How was it his parents truly believed he wanted to leave what was shaping up to be one of his best summers ever to sit in a car for hours and hours just to visit some roving museum?

His mood turned from grey to black as the beautiful sophomore Ella replied to both Chris and his friend to "grow up."

How was he going to convince Ella that it was him she needed if he was gone for two weeks? All of the ingenious plots that came to mind did not provide the outcome he was looking for. In teenage time two weeks was enough to create a meaningful relationship, have intimate relations, and break up in a cataclysmic scene of drama and tears.

He banged the computer desk with frustration, causing the wall to shake and something in his sister's room next door to fall and break. He waited for the shriek and was not disappointed when her door slammed and his flew open.

"What arc you doing jerk!" Sara landed in front of him like a virago. "That was my picture of Ryan you just broke! You are going to replace it Chris!

Sara turned and slammed out of the room as quickly as she'd come. Chris rolled his eyes before turning them back to his computer screen.

***

Sara returned to her room with tears burning in her eyes. Her brother could be such a...such a...the only words she could come up with were never spoken in their house. Sara screeched in frustration. The picture frame she'd made in Home Ec. to house the picture she and Ryan had taken at prom lay at the bottom of her wastebasket next to her bed. She stomped her foot in frustration before looking at the picture now pinned to the corkboard above her computer desk.

Ryan was the first and only boy she'd truly loved. She'd had many crushes, but she now realized they were childish moments of admiration. What she and Ryan had was real. Maybe when she got back from her lame family vacation he and Sara would finally consummate their love.

Sara blushed at the thought, turning to the mirror on her closet door. She'd matured since her fifteenth birthday just a couple of months ago. Her bosom had finally grown past the first letter in the bra alphabet and she actually had hips and a waist now instead of looking like a pencil.

"Yes", she decided, "she was ready for a Ryan to see her naked."

Sara quickly looked at the door sure her mother had heard her thoughts. Her mom could read her like a book and it frustrated Sara. Chris got away with so much. If their mom and dad had even half an idea of what Chris did alone in his room on that computer…Aarghhh!

"Chris, Sara let's go!"

Sara, who'd expected her mother to come bursting in the door with a chastity belt jumped as her mother called to them from down the hall. She turned to the suitcase and travel bag on her bed and began shoving the remains of her clothing and toiletries into it.

Her thoughts were filled with Ryan, his kiss, his words of love, his small attempts to get to second base. She smiled to herself as she zipped her bags closed. Wasn't he going to be surprised when she returned?

With this thought in mind, Sara gave a satisfied grunt as she lifted her bags off the bed and headed out to the garage.

At that same moment her mother stood in her bathroom clutching the vanity and staring into the mirror. Annie was still attractive enough for a woman in her early forties. All the hallmarks of aging were beginning to introduce themselves to her along her forehead and around her eyes. Gravity was giving her bra a run for its money, and her waistline was unwilling to bend to her stomach crunches.

For an infinitesimal moment, Annie considered running far away as lyrics from an old eighties song began to pound fear into her like Satan's drum; "This is not my beautiful house…and the days go by."

This happened to Annie frequently. Fear, like a wild beast that circled her home waiting to devour them all, would settle on her making her a slave to its voice.

She lifted her head and prayed. "Take it Lord".

"Give it to Me Annie." she heard softly in her heart.

And here is where her battle rested. She wanted to give it to Him. She didn't want to be burdened with this fear that made her want to run. She was afraid however if she gave it to Him, the hurts and fears that made her who she was would be banished, and she didn't know who'd she'd become.

Tears streaked her face. The frustration of this on-going battle was starting to wear on her. She turned the water on and splashed her face. Resolving to be happy, she turned and grabbed her bags from the bedroom and making a final sweep of the house she joined her family.

She knew as she stepped into the garage that her smile was overly bright. She could feel her face stretch into a manic smile, and tried to take it down a notch. She didn't want her family to know she'd been crying. Seeing John's exasperation when these moods came on her had taught her to keep it to herself.

'Annie's Terror', as John called it, was an unresolved fear Annie had struggled with since her childhood. Boogeymen sneaking into her room at night, holding her and touching her…The terror crept up on her like the family friend who had caused her fear.

John's struggle with it came from her inability to let down her guard, to always wait for the bad to come. Her inability to trust completely had thus far hindered their ability to discover the intimacy of marriage they both so craved, even after twenty years.

"Let's get this show on the road!" John was excited as he encouraged everyone to leave their bags at the back and get settled in the car. Twenty minutes later all of their bags and camping gear was packed and they were ready to hit the road.

The Beloved family reviewed their checklist one last time, loaded themselves into their SUV, and started on an adventure so fraught with danger and fear Annie would have laughed at her childhood fear right then, and spat in its face.

***

Sitting behind the wheel of their GMC Denali, John loaded their destination into the GPS.

They were heading out across the country leaving their lovely, albeit small, suburban home in San Diego, California and heading to the great state of Virginia on the east coast.

This was an educational vacation John had conceived, after reading an article in a Journal regarding the Shroud of Tourin. He had been intrigued with the debate that raged around the Shroud's authenticity.

His secret hope was the trip would entice his children to run from the temptations the world was shoving at them daily and run towards the only promise of hope left in a world sliding into chaos and sin.

When Annie and he had married they were what the church might label 'backsliding' Christians. They were both born again but had allowed their fears and doubts to stifle the freedom that came from a personal relationship with Christ.

Over the years however, through many life crises (Chris' near death experience with infant pneumonia, Annie's "Terrors" and the death of John's father), their faith had stretched, grown, and matured.

When their children were born John and Annie experienced a supernatural conviction to raise them as the word commanded, but the world was at war with them now that their children were young adults, making this vacation more important than ever.

Over the next ten days, the Beloved family would wind their way through the U.S. until they reached their destination where a travelling museum of the Shroud was available for viewing.

John, whose job as an engineer for a national pipe manufacturing company never led to any great discoveries of truth, was extremely excited to see the museum and prayed his wife and children would share his enthusiasm.

His own amateur studies led him to believe that not only was the Shroud what it claimed to be, but there were implications to the shroud that would provide his children new incentive to cling to the salvation of Christ crucified and raised from the dead.

.   The car eased out of the driveway and Sara's boyfriend Ryan stood on the lawn watching them go. He waved to Sara and blew her a kiss.

John watched this love scene from the rearview mirror and grimaced. Sara and Ryan had been dating for a little over 6 months.

His daughter was a wonder. She was beautiful, intelligent and compassionate, but Ryan was trouble. He knew through his wife that Sara was on the verge of sleeping with Ryan if she hadn't already.

Annie was such a great mom. He knew that she was wise and that she would envelop Sara in her sage advice (or take a stick to her). Either way, John up to this point tried very hard not to get too involved, but not to distance himself completely.

Outside of time

We were not allowed to love.

Adore yes.

Worship yes.

But love was not an emotion we were given access too. Somehow this one thing, this one emotion, was relevant to being outside of time and His will.

The vine and graft (or VG) as they were discussed in these circles always assumed that choice was the thing that most lusted after, but that in fact was not the case.

If not allowed to choose, then how had so many fallen? How had so many decided to rebel?

The Light, the Son of Dawn, as is known in these circles, remains the everlasting dawn of the rebellion.

How else could the Light rebel unless by conscious choice?

It seemed a very basic thing to comprehend. Though most in these circles give little respect or credit to the VG.

Just watching those along the Time Dimension showed their incomprehensible need to repeat themselves over and over.

Creating and recreating the same cities, cultures, gods, and wars. So easy to predict really which meant that The Light was consistently on the winning side in all matters earthbound; A fact that was represented to IAM over and over again with not the smallest bit of irreverence and self-satisfaction.

It could be said that the Light continued this irreverence and self-satisfaction with the same repetitive nature outside time as the VG did inside.

This would never be said face to face of course, only in quiet dark corners, where sound travelled at an equation not yet even come into the hearts and minds of you know who.

The "Time of times" escalates. In these circles, expectations for the full assault are high.

After millennium, which by comparison is a small amount of waiting, the stage begins to form.

A plan so long in the making could hardly be contained here outside time. It stretched and pulled and groaned with anticipation. It was, ironically, much like the VG and all living things, ever hopeful of their triumph.

Chapter 2

June 11, 2001 Beloved Family Road Trip –
Well the Beloved Road Trip is well underway.
We started out on Interstate 15 and travelled
north taking Highway 395 through the Sierra
Nevada's.
John did such a wonderful job mapping the trip,
I think the car could have driven the family to
our first stop in Reno on its own...
                    ***
"Annie! Wake up! Annie wake up!"
Sleep tumbled unwillingly away from Annie as she was pushed without consent into consciousness.
"What?! ...John, what is it?" it was out of her mouth even before she was aware it.

As she opened her eyes she found John leaning over her, his face very close to hers.

"Babe, you were screaming!" his whisper was urgent as he bent down and pressed his lips to hers.

"I most certainly was not screaming!"
She was still dazed as she pushed her husband away and sat up swinging her legs over the side of the bed. "I was dreaming quite pleasantly about our drive up here. I was writing my thoughts in my journal right before you shook me awake."

Annie looked over her shoulder annoyed at her husband but pulled up short on her intent to berate him for waking her so abruptly.

He was stricken, and pale, and...and... frightened?

Annie searched her time reference for a moment. When had she ever seen John looking so terrified? When nothing came to mind she turned around to face him and put her hand on his balding head.

"What is it honey? What's the matter?"

John sagged under her touch just a little, and then stood agitated, putting distance between them.   How could he tell her? He wasn't sure if he was really awake.

He'd fallen asleep exhausted from the driving, stopping, and pictures of the first day of their vacation. He'd been awakened abruptly by a scream that still wrung over and over him like brackish water wrung from a filthy t-shirt; a scream that still seemed to echo off the walls of their hotel room.

It was Annie, his Annie who'd screamed.

He knew her, he knew her voice, and the agony in it was like someone stretching her on a rack.

The terror in her plea had driven him instantly mad. He hadn't been able to find her or save her! His hands still shook and he thought he might vomit. What happened?

"What happened?" he voiced it in a whisper like an accusation.

Annie swung around to face him. "Babe, it was a bad dream!"

She leaned toward him to wrap her arms around him and reassure him, but he uncharacteristically stuck his arms out in a resistive motion and pushed her back.

Hurt registered in her eyes, but her face was angry.

"What the heck do you think you're doing Jonathan Beloved!?" She glanced quickly toward the closed door of the room where Sara and Chris were no doubt fast asleep. She stood and took a deep breath trying to calm herself.

"John, please talk to me, I don't understand."

John turned toward Annie and she saw tears in his eyes.

"Good", she thought grumpily, "You should feel bad".

His next words however changed her heart.

"Annie", his voice quavered and his hands shook, "You were hurt and I couldn't get to you. You were screaming in agony and I couldn't find you".

Annie's anger deflated slowly as she tried to calm his fears.

"You were dreaming! I'm obviously o.k. honey." Her condescension apparent, she continued in a loud whisper, "You really didn't need to put your hands on me".

Her words appeared to catalyze him as he rushed around the bed to where she stood.

"Your right, I'm sorry babe".

John took her into his arms for a quick hug, but then just as quickly as the embrace began it was over as he pushed her abruptly away and turned his back to her.

"This wasn't a dream Annabelle! I swear I heard you like I hear you now".

She felt a little chill run up her spine at his words, but more at his use of her given name.

She'd never, in their entire married life, seen her husband look as he did now; paralyzed with fear, eyes tearstained red, and to her dismay, unable to look at her.

She approached again, taking a different tact this time. Softly, she lifted her hands to his shoulders and began rubbing them trying to help him relax.

"Alright John, I'm o.k." her soothing tone made his shoulders sag. "It's just a little after two in the morning, let's get some sleep and we can discuss it tomorrow o.k.?"

John nodded his head and started toward the door connecting their room to their children's. "What are you doing babe?"

He turned to reply and she was relieved to see her John was back.

"I'm just going to check on the kids".

That was better, that was the hubby she knew. Annie's smile was sleepy as she eased herself back onto the bed and under the covers.

Her respite was brief however, for just as she laid her head on the lovely sleep inducing pillow, John's cry of "What the...?!" made her leap from the bed and scramble to the second bedroom.

As she stopped short at the doorway, she saw what had caused her husband to cry out. Her babies were gone.

Chapter 3

June 12, 2001 Downtown Reno 2:00 am
 Sara took a step nearer to her brother.
 He stood tall and handsome in the neon light of the casinos.
 His dirty blond hair, sky blue eyes, and swaggering confidence no one deserved, made him appear eight feet tall.
 There were lights everywhere and Sara was just a little overwhelmed. Chris on the other hand seemed excited. He'd had a great time so far scoping out drunken young women in each small casino and bar they passed.
 "Why did she let Chris talk her into doing these things?"
 Her big brother was so charismatic so like their mom. He smiled and people offered him a job. He told a joke and they wanted to be his best friend.
 It had never been like that for Sara.
 At five foot eight with a lithe and sometimes gawky build and large brown eyes like her father's she was shy and introspective. At least that's what her mother told her. Sometimes however she just wanted to shout back in her face "I AM WORTHY OF YOUR PRAISE!"
 Sara knew in her heart this wasn't fair even as the thought vanished from her mind. Her mom praised all of her efforts, even when she felt those efforts were not in Sara's best interest.
 Somehow though, when it was the four of them, or even around Sara's extended family, it seemed like Chris was the star. He commanded everyone's attention.
 "Maybe that is why Ryan seemed like such a blessing" she pondered as she followed her

brother. When she was with Ryan she was all that existed. She was important. She was the star. She shook her head troubled. "Where had that thought come from?"

Chris turned to look at his sister who was lagging. He knew his sister so well. He knew more than anything Sara loved to embrace every experience, to live in the moment; whether she was at Church singing Christ's praises, or walking their dog at home. Sara loved to just soak it all in and 'make memories'. He also knew she got that from their mother, although he'd never say so to her.

He on the other hand felt ready to explode. Sara had it so easy. Here he was facing adulthood and he had no idea what he wanted to do with his life. The pressure was already on for him to choose a college, choose his profession, make his parents proud. These decisions occupied most of his time, and he admitted to himself, girls occupied the rest. He wanted so desperately to live up to the expectations of his family, to not disappoint. Fear would wrap around him constantly. Failure would laugh at him. His escape had become women. They asked for so little and gave so much pleasure in return.

A still small voice whispered to his heart, "its empty."

Chris knew that voice. It was God. Sometimes he allowed it to change his perspective, a lot of the time he pushed it away.

This time he shoved the voice away focusing once more on the bright lights that dazzled the sky around them. He'd talked his sister into this little adventure.

"Get your head in the game man."

When he'd first approached Sara after their parents had gone to bed, she'd balked.

"Oh no. You know mom's got some kinda supersonic radar. She'll know. She'll wake up and find out we're gone and then the rest of our summer will be over when we get home."

Chris just smiled sly.

"Come here and put your ear to the door."

Sara had growled in protest, but got up and joined her brother whose ear was already pressed to the door.

Their parents were indeed fast asleep. This was evidenced by their almost synchronized snoring. Dad's loud and snuffled, mom's quiet and buzzing.

She felt the spark of excitement shoot through her.

"Alright bro", Sara smiled conspiratorially; "let's see what Reno has to offer".

Thirty minutes later they were looking in cheap casinos watching tired players tied to machines with strings of hope.

"Woohoo, this is a blast!" Sara frowned hugging her arms to her chest as they paused at the Second Street intersection in the heart of Reno's downtown strip.

Outside of Time

I am Random.

I am the thresher of the tares known as humankind, or more appropriately, the sifter of men. It is only because permission could not be obtained, that "Saint Peter" does not lay sifted on my threshing room floor.

I started my ascent in these circles by creating... no must not use that word... (the Light   fancied   himself   the "creationist")...through might and an uncanny ability to illuminate Chaos' feeble attempts at destruction.

Chaos however is by definition, a disorder to order, lackluster at best in scope with no lasting value.

I have been the master of all acts of Random violence for it is my kingdom and purpose. Staged over and over within the VG's frame of reference (time) to appear disordered with no reason or sense of meaning, leaving brokenness almost impossible to heal.

I am Random.

Little boys run down, old women raped, little girls gone missing, whole families tortured, mutilated, and shot when they thought they were safe.

Randomly.

A tribute to the greatness of my work.

The Light has promised (looking upward for permission as it was said) to reveal my mastery at the time of times.

So now I wait at the corner of a street, lit by neon promises (illusionary at best) to crea...no to stage another masterpiece to hang on stars at the time of times.

Chris looked to the left and the right out of habit more than anything else as he and his sister waited for the light to change at the intersection where they stood.

The main drag of downtown Reno was pretty quiet. All of the people were huddled in the casinos looking for a miracle.

The light turned green and he turned to offer his hand to his sister to pull her across the street and was surprised to see a large shadow on the wall behind her.

He blinked rapidly as the shadow began to wave like heat off of pavement,

"Shimmering" he realized...

"No that couldn't be right...shimmering?"

He opened his mouth and pointed a finger behind his sister ready to tell her to turn around and look at the shadow and how it shimmered when a man stepped through it.

"Stepped through it?" his mind tried to compute, baffled.

His sister looked at him with a question in her eyes and a quirk to her lips as she started to turn and look at what had caused her brother to look so startled.

Just then the man who had stepped through the shadow lunged at Sara stepping up to her and pushing her to the ground with a shove to the middle of her back.

She made a gurgling noise as she fell and as the man moved back toward the shimmering Chris saw that he had dropped a stick on his sister's back. It stood poised in the middle of her back likes some kind of macabre ballerina and if Chris didn't know better he would have said it was laughing at him.

All of this happened like lightning. Flashing in front of him and then done.

Chris heard the thunder in his ears as he lunged for the man and swung his fist directly at his head, but the man was lightning too, and in a shimmering shadow, disappeared.

Chapter 4

Panic was the word both Annie and John would have used to name the hum that vibrated through both of them as they started down the hall to the elevator. They knew their kids were smart, and knew they generally exhibited common sense, but when they decided to do something that guaranteed swift retribution, they always went big. Now as they stood in a lonely elevator vestibule waiting for the ding to take them down to the casino, there was a charge of anger in the air.

John glanced at the number on the digital readout to see where the elevator was travelling from before glancing at Annie. She stood with her arms wrapped around her waist. Her hair was a mess and there were smudges of makeup under her eyes.

"She's amazing." Surprised by the thought, primarily because it did not feel like his own, John blurted. "You're amazing!"

Annie who'd been reviewing the events that had led to this after hours foray looked up surprised by her husband's comment.

"Thank you honey" was accompanied by a small puckered smile and a little laugh. "Unfortunately, I feel more like a zombie right now."

She rubbed her eyes and looked up at her husband, only to find him once again studying the red numbers descending above the elevator doors.

"John" came out a little harshly, and Annie changed her tone quickly when he looked down at her. "I'm scared."

Her husband reached out immediately pulling her to him. "Don't worry babe. We'll find them and they will be fine. They will have some sense smacked into them, and be on restriction til they graduate, but they will be fine."

His smile reassured her, and Annie hugged him tightly before the ding announcing their ride tickled the air. They moved into the elevator as one, still hugging each other close. The elevator was silent except for the announcement of the casino's "Super Buffet" through the speaker system. They reached the casino level with a bump and swish from the elevator's brakes.

As the doors opened John shook his head slightly. It was almost three in the morning now and the casino was alive. People walked by with long drinking glasses and money vouchers from the machines. As they stepped out into the action, John pulled Annie aside.

"Why don't you go look back toward the café and game room honey" he instructed. "I'll go look near the machines and we'll meet back here in ten minutes o.k.?"

Annie knew this was not a request but a game plan and she nodded and started back towards her sector. She laughed to herself at the thought. John had been in the Army as a young man and could run things with the precision of a drill sergeant at times.

John walked through what seemed like miles of glittering lights and pinging machines searching row upon row for his children. He did not find them. What he did find on this first night of their journey made him sad. Hundreds of people tied to lifeless machines like succubuses; waiting for a sinking ship to come in. He checked his watch. At least ten minutes had passed and he started back towards his wife's location.

He was about one hundred feet from the spot where he'd left her when he caught sight of her. She was talking to an elderly black gentleman.

Annie loved the elderly. The Lord had put a soft spot in her heart for them and she would often stop to talk to them in the store or when she went out on her nightly walks. The older gentleman she spoke to now was a bit of a surprise.

He looked different from the other patrons of the casino. He wore a beautiful multicolored floor-length caftan which appeared to be made of silk and was open in the front. Underneath he wore a soft cotton shirt and pants the color of sand and held a cane or staff that he leaned upon.

John's first thought upon seeing him was "royalty."

As he moved closer, weaving between chairs and machines, he could not take his eyes off his wife.

She appeared to have been transformed into a human beacon. Her face shown so brightly it was if she'd stuck a flashlight in her mouth. Her features were barely distinguishable, and he found the closer he got the more brightly Annie seemed to shine.

As he moved, he looked absently around the ceiling above where she stood, expecting or perhaps hoping, to find the source of the light.

It was if beams were shooting from all sides of her, almost like…like fire!

He rushed forward holding his hand in front of his face to shield it from the light and reached her just as the elderly gentleman turned and shuffled away.

The stranger, John noted, leaned heavily on a beautifully carved ivory cane with the head in the shape of a cross that curled into an upside down "U".

He reached for Annie from behind, and had just begun to ask who the gentleman was, when Annie turned to him and he was knocked back by the radiance enveloping her.

"Glorious Glory!" John lifted his hand and let a trembling finger trace her face before shaking his head to clear the dizzy laughter that was threatening. Instead he looked at the ceiling again for some source of trick lighting.

"Why are you shining?!" his mind screamed, "Our children are missing!"

He was finally able to gather his thoughts and asked "Who was that nice looking man?"

Annie, he saw, couldn't immediately respond because of some unknown joy she was experiencing. It radiated from her eyes and hair and fingertips and John was stunned when he realized Annie bursting and becoming an orbital star would not surprise him at this moment. When she finally could speak her words were soft with wonder.

"Babe, let's go back to the room and I will tell you the most extraordinary thing that just happened." John looked at her as if she had an eye missing, and he shook her slightly.

"Annie, we have to find the kids! What are you talking about?" His vehemence caused her joy to stumble ever so slightly.

It was funny and sad as he watched the shine begin to fade, and he was sorry for it and wanted to bring it back, but it was too late. She turned her face into his chest and wrapped her arms around him.

"It's o.k., it's all o.k., let's get up to the room, please John."

**

John slipped the card key into the slot and opened the door letting Annie step in first and following after as the door swung shut behind him.

"What's going on Annie?" He needed to know and asked as he ran a hand down his face to smudge away his fear.

"John, sit down."

He gazed at his wife a little offended, but backed toward the bed sitting automatically as the edge caught the back of his knees.

"Annie, talk to me."

Annie sat next to her husband, curling one leg beneath her, in order to angle herself toward him.

She sandwiched one of his large hands between the two of hers, and leaned in closer taking a deep breath.

"I'm not really sure how to explain", she began, a thin veil of composure conspicuous in her voice, "so please just bear with me okay?"

At John's nod, she continued.

"That lovely older gentleman I was speaking with approached me as I was running around like a mad woman through the game room." Her arms began gesturing wildly as she spoke to prove her point.

"John it was incredible! "That lovely gentleman appeared out of nowhere!"

She smiled brightly wiping tears from her eyes, and the room illuminated around her before she began speaking again.

"He touched my arm and I was suddenly and completely overcome by this sense of…of stillness…of calmness!"

Closing her eyes she reached back into that moment. As John looked on, a beautiful radiance began to emanate from her face and through her body again. He reached out trying to capture it, when Annie opened her eyes.

She smiled at him as his hand dropped back to his lap, and he smiled back. Her joy was infectious!

"That nice old man said 'what's wrong little lady?' and the tone and timber of his words made me laugh out loud, like he was sharing a joke with me. I became flustered, and I didn't want to go into the whole story so I just said, "Our children have decided to take an evening walk, and we don't know where they've gone".

At this point in her story, Annie leapt off the bed like she'd been poked. She spun around and instead of seeing the fear he was feeling, John saw she was almost giddy.

"That man looked at me and said "Sara and Christopher are fine Annie".

John reached for her to pull her back to the bed to sit down, but Annie just danced away from him. Literally danced!

"John, that nice man, whose name is Michael, knew our names, and he told me that the children had just fought their first battle, but there would be many more to come and that we needed to be prepared!"

"When he said it I wasn't frightened!" "I knew he was right, I just knew."

Full brilliance like a ball of light!…and John once again looked for a source …although he knew on some level of consciousness that it came from within her, but was not quite ready to accept it yet.

"He told me where to find them, and that they were safe. John, it was the hand of the Lord! I felt it, felt it in my spirit!"

John was feeling as if he'd just stepped into a parallel dimension. Annie had never spoken like this before!

"What is going on?!" his mind screamed before his wife's words finally penetrated. "Where are they Annie? Where are the kids?"

Downtown Reno 2:40 am

Chris could not stop his forward motion after lunging at the man who'd attacked his sister and continued falling. He saw that he would land directly over Sara, shoving the handle of whatever protruded from her back deeper. In the panic of his fall, he rolled sideways to avoid her and the right side of his head cracked the curb.

Just as the stars vanished from his eyes he thought, "I've killed my sister", then blackness embraced him like a long lost friend".

Chapter 5

"They're in their room!" Annie laughed. Then seeing the disbelief in her husband's eyes, she repeated herself emphatically, careful to enunciate each word.

"They… are… in… their… room!"

John looked at her as if she'd lost her mind, but Annie didn't care. She'd been given a glimpse, a 'This Present Darkness' look at the forces of light and shadow playing out.

She was giddy and watched as John leapt off the bed and ran toward the connecting door. He threw it open causing it to bang loudly against the wall and almost followed after it in his panic.

Annie was right! Their kids were both in their own beds fast asleep and undisturbed by the noise caused by their father's hurried entrance.

John ran over to Chris' bed shaking his son violently. "You've got some explaining to do!" he screamed as he yanked him from his bed.

He grabbed Chris' arm as he turned and hurried over to Sara's bed. She had not so much as twitched. John began shaking his daughter, yelling at her to wake up, but she just lay there unaware of his efforts.

"Dad, dad! Please listen to me, Dad please."

The rushing blood in John's ears began to subside and he finally heard his son pleading with him. He turned to find he was grasping Chris' left bicep in a death grip.

He dropped his son's arm like a red hot poker, and stepping away from his daughter's sleeping form, sat heavily on Chris' bed. His son's questions chilled him.

"How did you find us? Why isn't Sara at the hospital? What is happening?"

John heard the tears in his son's voice, a sound he hadn't heard in several years. He looked up ready to apologize, ready for an explanation only to find Annie had cocooned their son in her mother's embrace.

She walked Chris over to his bed and sat him down gently next to his father.

"Please son, tell your father and I what happened".

Chris looked up, his gaze resting on each of them in turn.

"They will never believe me, where do I even begin?" his brain felt fuzzy and confused. He rose slowly and went over to Sara's bed. Stooping he kissed his sister's forehead. She was still warm.

"Oh thank you Jesus!" ran through him like a song, as the verge of tears revisited his eyes.

Out loud he whispered, "She's o.k., she's o.k."

Chris peeled the covers back from Sara who lay on her stomach, her hands folded by her head.

A blood stain the size of a grapefruit lay in a circle at the small of her back. His parents saw the blood and his father pushed his trembling son out of the way.

Annie wrapped her arms around Chris peering over his shoulder. He did begin to cry then, silently shaking as tears of relief and fear ran down his cheeks. His parents were here now. They would know what to do.

He watched his dad lifted Sara's cotton T-Shirt up her back. It stuck to her skin where the blood had pooled. All three of the Beloveds gasped when they saw the wound. To Chris' great relief it was actually more of a scrape than a wound, but it was deep. It looked like she'd lost half an inch of skin just above her tailbone.

John looked up at his son with a question and a hint of anger in his eyes. Chris, shamed, looked down at his mother who was looking at him like she was going to laugh any minute.

In a low voice, smattered with deep breaths, he told his parents as precisely as he could what had happened at Virginia and Second Street. He chose to leave out the shimmering and flashing, and only described a man appearing from the shadows. He also chose not to remember or mention the eyes of the man, which had taken up two-thirds of his face, or the grayish color of his skin.

Outside of Time

I am Random.

A very important assignment completed and surely the Random name will be vaunted above those in these circles.

The fear and terror on young Mr. Beloved's face was an elixir that created a high as strong as opium. A treasure, stored up for the time of times.

Movement and shadow, wailing and gnashing of teeth; The Deceiver of Nations stands tall as a mountain. (Always one to make an entrance is this one).

Perhaps a reward was in order, perhaps a new arrival to torture?

"You've failed."

Though communicated quietly, it crushed and ripped open the dermas to expose a life beater which was slowly squeezed and chewed on as a reminder of the missed opportunity.

Sara was still a little drowsy. She lay on the table of St. Mary's Emergency Care just a few blocks from their hotel.

She was confused and nervous. "What had happened?"

She remembered getting dressed to sneak out with Chris and then nothing. It frightened her because she was not sure why she could not remember.

Her father sat next to her, his arm resting lightly on her bed, as he looked back and forth between her mom and brother.

"Dad, I want to go home." came out as a raspy whisper. Her father had to lean in to hear her, "what honey?"

Sara resisted the urge to roll her eyes. Her father was deaf in his right ear, but refused to wear a hearing aid. "I want to go home dad, I don't like this road trip"

"Sara, we can't turn around now baby. The doctor said you'll be fine, but a little sore. Maybe you'll think twice about leaving the room without permission hmm?"

Sara's cheeks flamed, not with embarrassment, but anger.

"I told you I don't even remember leaving the room! How can I get in trouble for something I don't even remember?"

Her father patted her hand, which she hated. As the youngest, she was always treated like a child. She was sixteen! She'd almost had sex! She was not a baby! Tears started to roll down her eyes. Typical!

If Chris had gotten hurt they probably would have care-flighted him to the nearest ultra-specialist hospital. What did she get? A backed up emergency room, a doctor with smelly breath, and a promise of having to sit against the wound on her back over the next eight hour leg of their trip.

Where the injury on her back had come from was still a mystery. She had little fragmented pictures that flashed around behind her eyes in random order: Chris holding out his hand, confused and terrified, watching people at the machines in the casinos, getting dressed to sneak out. That was all and it didn't make any sense to her.

The doctor said the small abrasion on her back looked worse than it was. It had taken only three stitches to close it. When the doctor lectured her and Chris about playing with swords, she had laughed and looked at her brother ready to share the humor, but he was staring wide-eyed at the doctor and beads of sweat had gathered on his upper lip.

"Swords Doctor?" her mother's voice was lined with disbelief.

"Well", the doctor continued, "it looks like the wound was made by a sharp blade approximately two inches wide, but broken to the quick, which accounts for the jagged scrape rather than a deep puncture wound.

I am sure your children can explain it better than I in any event. Keep the wound dry and change the bandage every other day for ten days, then give it some air. You folks have a good vacation." Dr. Bad Breath finished as he gave a small wave and left.

There was silence for the space of a heartbeat.

When John Beloved spoke his voice was soft and deadly calm.

"This is the strangest night of my life and I am so angry right now discussion is not an option, understood?" No one uttered a word.

"We are going back to the hotel, having a much needed family prayer and getting some sleep." He stood and paced the small area looking at each of them in turn.

"Then tomorrow, we are going to sit down to a lovely breakfast from room service and have a serious discussion before we begin our next leg of the trip." "Agreed?"

Annie, Chris, and Sara knew of course that this was rhetorical, but they nodded their heads just the same.

Chris and John stepped out of the cubicle to allow Annie to help Sara dress.

They left the hospital hunched together like a football team getting ready to huddle. Sara watched the lights go by and kept thinking, it's the light... the shimmering.

Outside of Time

"Failed?" It was incomprehensible.

After punching through, and with the element of surprise, it had really just been a matter of using the instrument of death directly and precisely to sever her spine at the L5.

The Dawn of Rebellion never blinked. Reaching around and pulling the wicked implement of destruction from behind, and holding it up to the glow falling from tall rigid shoulders.

"What is this?"

It was a broken destructive aid is what it was.

Confusion, usually such a comfort in these circles spoke up,

"It is broken or snapped, it's definitely broken I bel...

"Shut Up" a command accompanied by a sharp and searing pain to Confusion's protruding eye.

"I AM has sent intervention, Gabriel more than likely. This is going to become very complicated. This vermin family, particularly the girl, offer the highest probability for a loss in this decade."

"Exterminate them."

"Failure will not be tolerated."

Spoken in a whisper it was, barely above audible. The screeching, keening wail that followed lent credence to the statement.

Chapter 6

June 14, 2001 Beloved Family Road Trip
We had a wonderful prayer back at the hotel, and Sara complained very little about her back as we started toward Utah.

John seems very quiet, so I've kept to myself, mostly by admiring the landscape. I just haven't felt the time is right to explain to him how GREAT I feel about this trip.

I know the Lord has a plan for John during this trip, but he hasn't revealed it to me.

Chris is very subdued. He told his father and I that what happened to Sara was his fault. I tried to reassure him, but being seventeen, he would not listen, and so I've turned it over to our Heavenly Father.

We've just passed Wendover and the air seems electric. There's a storm coming.
***

"Dad, I need a bathroom break", Chris squirmed around in the backseat to emphasize his point.
John looked in the rearview mirror and laughed at his son's pained expression.

"Alright, we should be out of the Salt Flats in about ten minutes, hang in there son".

John looked around at the vast expanse where high speed records were made, pointing out the Morton Salt plant to his family.

As his gaze rested on the most distant point of the flats, he noticed the air begin to shimmer.

"Shimmer?" the question barely had time to move from his mind to his eyes as, blinking rapidly, he watched a low profile truck pop through the air!

"What the?...", he felt the wheel jerked out of his hands and turned quickly to see Annie turning the Denali to miss an on-coming sign.

"Had he drifted?" his heart beat an arrhythmia and he gulped in air staring straight ahead and trying not to slam on the brakes.

"What are you doing John Beloved? Are you trying to get us killed?"

Annie's face was flushed with fear and anger as she looked at her husband.

"I, I'm not sure what just happened", he said looking at his wife with embarrassment.

"I was looking at the flats, and the air was shimmering, and I saw...I saw..." John's words drifted off.

Annie looked at him with concern.

Fortunately neither turned around or they would have been more frightened than concerned.

Their son was clutching the seatbelt across his chest, and he didn't need to stop for the bathroom anymore.

June 15, 2001 Beloved Family Road Trip

"Well, with the exception of the near collision in Utah, the Beloved family road trip was uneventful. John gave me a good scare, but would not speak about it, although he did keep looking in the rearview mirror as we travelled through Wyoming and Nebraska.

Sara was extremely excited when her father asked her to take over the driving in Wyoming. She didn't complain about her back once in the four hours she was behind the wheel.

Chris of course pouted in the back seat. He was humiliated about his accident and refused to talk to anyone about it. We should be arriving at our destination in two more days, God willing.

We've had another good family prayer (isn't it funny how we do that when things are scary?). The Beloved family has prayed together more in the last few days than we have for a very long time. "Thank you Lord!"

Outside of Time

How the VG travelled in such low technology contraptions for thousands of miles goes beyond comprehension.

Energy, neither understood nor considered by the VG, fuels our travel dimensionally and along the space / time continuum.

Energy expelled from a single breath, energy which gave a superior creation the knowledge to manipulate the universe! Knowledge to be shared with those we've enslaved for the master's purposes and to our master's end.

Digressing, digressing.

I follow, I hunt, I cause, I masterfully execute. They will perish, the Great Dragon wills it, and so it must be.

***

Prior to their trip, Annie had mapped out every campsite and motel on their route.

Tonight in Nebraska they would stay at the lovely Gothenburg campsite near Kearney.

She had reserved a one room 'Kampy Kabin' at this particular campsite, which included a queen-size air bed and a bunk bed. This was, in Annie's opinion, much better than sleeping in a tent on the ground.

Everyone was exhausted. They had travelled over eight hundred miles and were all ready for some sleep.

A heavy storm began about five miles from their destination. A sleeting rain followed them as they found their cabin and began unloading their gear for the night.

"O.k. everyone, unroll your sleeping bags, and let's get some shut eye." John yawned as he smiled at his glaze-eyed clan. It had been a fairly uneventful drive, which was a welcome change from their trip thus far.

Annie and Sara were grabbing pajamas, toiletries, and toothbrushes as he spoke. "We'll be right back honey" Annie told her husband before pecking him on the lips and heading with her daughter to the camp restrooms. John and Chris took the opportunity to change into their sleep clothes while the girls were gone.

"You alright Chris?" The question was emphasized with a swat to his son's leg. John watched in silence as Chris jumped onto the top bunk. When his son's head came up so he could look his father in the eye, John was surprised to see Chris on the verge of tears.

John laid his hand on his arm. "You're not still upset about the accident in the car...."

"No Dad!" Chris interrupted before his father could bring the whole sordid incident up again. "I have to tell you something and I just don't know how to do it".

John's face became solemn. This must be serious. Chris, who was usually so laid back, seemed wound up like a helicopter wrist rocket.

"Just take your time son, tell me what's on your mind".

"Dad", Chris began, and hiccupped back the quiver in his voice. "What happened with Sara and me…"

John held up a hand to stop him, "It's fine son, it's over now".

"Dad! You need to hear this!" Chris had never in his life spoken so boldly to his father.

John sat back on the queen air mattress and looked up into his son's eyes. Yes, he could see that he did have to hear this.

"Alright son, let's have it".

Chris closed his eyes and recounted in detail exactly what had happened when he and Sara stood on the street corner in Reno. John's heart plummeted as his eldest child described the 'shimmering'.

John's mind seemed to go blank for the space of about five seconds. He was at a loss. He did not have a lot of experience, well actually no experience, in dealing with supernatural phenomena.

The closest he could ever remember coming to a world turned upside down was his father's death. God had jumped into his life at that time like a heroic paratrooper mowing through his depression and bringing him into the light again. He was beginning to understand that some decisions were going to have to be made. He needed to speak to his wife.

"Chris, I believe you." John stood abruptly seeing the look of relief on his oldest child's face.

"I believe you son" he said again. "Something extraordinary has taken hold of this trip. The Lord appears to be…I don't know…activating us."

John turned suddenly back to his son, their faces just inches apart, "I saw the shimmering you described." The confession came in a whisper, "when we were in the Salt Flats I saw the air shimmer and a truck pop through the air, but I thought I must be seeing things."

At the look of relief on his son's face, John started to say he thought they should be extremely cautious and not get mom…Mom! And Sara! John lunged for the door to the cabin and Chris was right behind him.

They were running in pitch black and pouring rain toward the light that signaled the bathrooms when a scream rent the air. As they ran into the light that surrounded the restrooms, John and Chris froze in terror at the sight they slammed into.

Annie stood with her back against the cinder blocks of the bathrooms, her arms thrust out toward a tall man whose features were hidden by the shadows.

Sara crouching behind her was screaming hysterically, "Help us Lord!" over and over.

John and Chris took all this in in an instant.

John rushed into action, moving forward to help his wife; he yelled back to Chris "Get your sister!"

Annie, small cries of despair escaping her lips, was struggling with the man from the shadows as he attempted to plunge a large sword like object down through her chest.

The blade gleamed in the fluorescent lighting, and John had a millisecond to see a ten inch blade with a hook on the end attached to a jewel crusted hilt. The creature pulled back the blade from Annie's grasp, gathering momentum for another downward thrust.

John watched this all as he moved like a man traversing quicksand. Just as he reached Annie's back, and was about to push her out of the way, Annie shouted in a voice that came from the recesses of her soul, "JESUS, Help us!"

Instantly, as if someone had turned on a giant light, the whole campsite was illuminated and the attacker was revealed.

It was not a man that stood over his wife, it was….John could not grasp it…it was a grotesque caricature of some human-like life form.

At least seven feet tall, its' long arms protruded from the base of its neck, covered in what could only be described as skin the color and texture of a squid; grey and greasy. Skin, John noted in his shock, alive and crawling; as if captured souls were nourished like parasites by the evil that emanated from the creature's form.

Blank eyes filled the entire front of its face, eyes devoid of life, yet filled with menace and hate.

Those eyes winced as the grounds illuminated, stopping the blade in mid swing. Screaming a tirade of filth, it disappeared with a shimmering flash.

In the silence that followed, the Beloved family stood frozen, as if a film reel had paused or broken. Sara squatted on the ground near the outdoor cleaning station, Chris had his arm wrapped tightly around her and appeared to be praying. Annie still had her eyes shut and her arms up as if the reel might be fixed and the scene begin again.

John mentally shook away his fear and rage and rushed toward Annie grabbing her roughly and squeezing her in a tight embrace. "I...I...I" was all that would come out of her mouth and John, believing shock was setting in, took charge.

"Chris bring your sister, stay close to me".

John gently pulled Annie toward their cabin and turned to Chris as they approached their campsite and the cabin. "Stay here with them" he ordered as he walked up the two steps to the small porch of the cabin and opened the porch screen.

He slowly lifted the bar to open the door, and pulled quickly on it, bursting into the cabin. He began making swift turns around the cabin with his fists raised when he heard laughter outside. He turned to see Annie standing between their children clenching her sides as she doubled over.

John rushed out to his wife, terrified she was losing her mind. He attempted to take her into his arms but she'd fallen to her knees continuing to laugh uncontrollably. After several moments, Annie looked up with tears running down her face and hiccupped back another bout of the giggles.

"John, if you could have seen what you looked like just now!" Even as she said it she felt the edge of madness grasping at her and took a deep reviving breath. John, sensing a lull in her hysteria, took Annie by her arm and nodded to their son to take the other. Together they pulled her to her feet.

"Come on guys let's get inside and lock ourselves in." Chris' voice was low as he let his mother's weight sag so she was leaning heavily on his dad. Letting go of her, he grabbed his sister around the shoulders and pulled her inside.

The Beloveds huddled around each other in the small cabin, each giving and receiving reassurance. John finally spoke into the silence, keeping his voice steady and asking the question they all desperately wanted answered.

"Annie, honey, do you have any idea what that thing was, or why it was trying to kill you?" The words sounded so foreign he almost began laughing hysterically himself.

Annie, seeing her husband on the precipice she was just returning from, knew that she needed to be strong right now. Stronger she realized, than she'd ever been. Because what she really wanted, what her mind, soul, and body craved was to curl up in a ball on the bed, stick her thumb in her mouth and go to sleep. She knew in her heart however this wasn't even a remote possibility.   Instead she lifted her eyes to meet those of her husband and children and in an unsteady voice began to explain what had happened.

"Sara and I went into the bathroom and set our things on the counter. We were both getting ready to brush our teeth.   We kept hearing a faint scratching sound in the last stall, you know the handicapped one?"

Sara's eyes were clenched tightly shut as she listened to her mother, but John and Chris nodded understanding. Annie took a deep breath and continued.

"Sara and I both glanced over at the stall. I was just thinking a mouse or something might have gotten into the restroom you know?" she asked rhetorically, looking towards her daughter for confirmation. Her daughter just continued to sit with her eyes tightly clenched, silent.

"That's when the door was flung open and that…that…that…"

John put his arm around his wife's shoulder and rubbed his hand up and down her back trying to comfort her.

"It's o.k. honey, take your time", John whispered softly, as he bent and kissed her forehead.

Annie heaved in a gulp of air before continuing, "That alien…, demon…, MONSTER lunged out of the stall and growled at us like a feral cat" her voice quavered and Annie seemed to shrink back from the memory, but went on, "It looked at me, but started for Sara, and I panicked and threw our hairdryer at it, grabbed Sara's hand and ran from the bathroom."

Annie wiped the tears from her eyes, "It was so dark when we got outside I must've run the wrong way. All of the sudden that thing just appeared with a pop in front of us, the air shimmered, and it popped in front of us!" Her eyes were wild when she looked up into the faces of her family. She dropped her head into her hands shaking it back and forth.

Chris swung his head toward his father at his mother's words, but his dad just shook his head slightly. "Not now" he mouthed kissing the top of Annie's head.

To Annie he asked, "Is there anything else honey? Did it speak to you?"

Annie remained silent for a heartbeat. When she finally spoke it was in a rushed breathless voice. She just wanted to finish the story as quickly as possible.

"It pulled out some kind of sword and grabbed at Sara, and that was when I was able to finally scream. I pushed Sara to the ground and turned to fight it when it spoke to me."   At this news the rest of her family turned and looked at Annie in surprise, even Sara who had been there.

"It did speak to you honey?" John asked with a bit of disbelief in his voice.

Annie would have normally taken offense but since the whole thing was so ludicrous, she just nodded her head and continued.

"It spoke in my head John, and it felt cold and desolate. I don't know how to explain it, but I could 'hear' the cold and desolation. I know that doesn't make any sense…" She trailed off, shaking her head back and forth, repeating "no sense, no sense."

John nudged her with his lips against her temple, "Baby, what did it say to you?"

She looked up into his eyes, lost and afraid, "It said, "give us the girl, your pain will be less. As if it truly believed we would just hand over Sara…"

At this Annie looked at her daughter. All of the color had drained from Sara's face and her little girl began to shake, terrified. Chris put his arm around his sister, and in a moment so precious none of them would ever forget it, quietly quoted the good word.

"No greater love has any man than this, that he would lay down his life for another", and then more emphatically, "No one is going to hurt my sister!"

"Alright", this trip is definitely become something more than any of us understood" John began and Annie sniffed loudly.

"Kids, Honey, I believe the Lord is leading us toward something, but I confess I'm at a loss as to what. I think we need to find some help." His confidence grew as he said it and he looked down into his wife's eyes. "Annie, tomorrow when we stop for breakfast I need you to find a Christian church. We need to speak to a pastor."

John worried his kids would revolt at his decision and demand tickets back home from the nearest airport, turned to them next, waiting for their response. He watched Chris and Sara grab each other's hands in silent confirmation before his son replied.

"Dad, we don't know what's going on either but we're a family and we need to see this through together." His son's voice was sure and strong and John had his first glimpse of his son as a man.

He couldn't remember a time in his life when he was more surprised or proud, than right now. He actually had to blink back tears, when Sara cuddled up next to him and said, "I'm scared daddy, but I know we need to do whatever the Lord's directing us to do. I'll feel a lot safer if we can get some help from a pastor."

Chapter 7

Annie Beloved Journal Entry
June 16, 2001 Beloved family road trip

Last night was the most frightening of my life. I truly believe that this trip has become about the Beloved's work for Christ rather than the Shroud of Turin, but John thinks they are all connected.

I was able to find a non-denominational Christian church in Grand Island just about fifty miles east of Kearney. The Loving Word Church seemed to pop out at me from my internet search.

Believing that this was the Lord's intervention I called and spoke to a Pastor Wallen. His voice soothed me at once when he picked up the phone, and so I am confident we are on the right road.

John is driving fast, but keeping an eye out for rogue vehicles (he and Chris both shared their encounters with the "shimmering"). Lord please get us to Pastor Wallen safely!

***

Pastor Wallen sat at his desk going through the church accounts prior to having his secretary, Ms. Wedner pay their monthly bills. They would be short again he knew.

The last storm that had blown through had caused a huge hole in the sanctuary roof, decimating the emergency fund. This meant the families who attended the church would have to look elsewhere for assistance.

Pastor Wallen's forty years of experience had taught him however, that Christ would provide for the needs of his people; he and the church were just a conduit the Lord used. He rubbed his hand over his eyes and face and thought briefly of the strange phone call he'd received.

Mrs. Beloved had been cryptic in her explanation of why her family needed to stop by and see him but she'd also sounded very scared. He'd felt in his spirit the Lord's admonition to speak with her and so he had invited she and her clan to see him when they arrived.

He picked up the phone and dialed Ms. Wedner's extension,

"Yes Pastor", his secretary, Ms. Wedner, smiled with her voice (Ms. Wedner was eighty years old).

"Lois, I'm expecting visitors, the Beloved family." he responded loudly (Ms. Wedner was a little hard of hearing), "Please show them in when they arrive."

"Yes, yes I'll show them right in", she said and he could hear the smile in her voice.

Ms. Wedner had worked for the Pastor as long as he'd worked at the church and had worked for previous pastors before him for over twenty years.

She worked as the secretary for free and did so with a joyous heart. It was her tithe she said since she believed giving her time was more fruitful than giving her money.

Her husband had died almost ten years before, and since then the pastor and Ms. Wedner had drawn close to each other as friends and as a brother and sister in Christ.

They spent so much time together, that a bit of nastiness had developed in the congregation. It had given him an opportunity to dust off his sermon on gossip however, bless God.

He visited her home weekly and tonight Ms. Wedner had promised some homemade chicken and dumplings. His stomach growled loudly in anticipation just before the intercom in his office rang.

"I have the Beloved family here to see you pastor", Ms. Wedner announced.

"Please send them right in" he replied, and stood to his feet to greet them.

The door opened slowly as Ms. Wedner led the small group into his office. She smiled at the group and asked who wanted coffee, or would anyone like cookies.

"Baked fresh today" she encouraged and the Beloved family nodded in unison.

"You too Pastor?" It was more of an inclusion than a question.

Pastor Wallen smiled at what appeared to be a nice normal family and then directed his gaze to his secretary. "Now Ms. Wedner, when have I ever refused your cookies" he replied, rubbing his belly. This caused instantaneous laughter from his guests, and he thought "good".

Rosy apples blushed on Ms. Wedner's papery cheeks which provided a glimpse of her youth, before she walked out of the room to gather refreshments.

John Beloved observed the scene between the Pastor and his secretary and smiled. He'd grown up in a church like this when he was young. His spirit was comforted by the familiarity, and he could see by looking at Annie and the kids, everyone was slowly letting their guards down for the first time in several hours.

John stuck his hand out, "Pastor Wallen", "I'm John Beloved, this is my wife Annie, and our children Chris and Sara." Each of them smiled in turn at the pastor and he nodded his head and smiled at each of them shaking the elder Mr. Beloved's hand.

Pastor Wallen showed them to a small round table with four chairs in the corner of his office. "Please, sit down, sit down."

The Beloved family seemed to move as one as they each found a seat. The Pastor resumed his seat behind the desk, but scooched it around with his feet so it faced the table. "So, Mr. Beloved..." he began before John quickly interrupted.

"Please Pastor call me John."

"Alright", the pastor smiled, "So John, and Beloved family, how can I be of assistance?"

The Beloved family members looked at each other and then all together looked at John. There was a collective sigh (or maybe more like a whoosh) from all of them, and then Mr. Beloved began to speak.

"Pastor, I have what I think today would constitute one of the more "normal" families. My wife and I have been married for a good long time, we have a modest home, our children attend the local public school, and we all attend our local church on Sunday". John paused, unsure of how to continue.

Pastor Wallen sensing John's distress held up his hand and smiled. "How about if we start with a prayer?" the pastor asked.

The Beloved family nodded their heads then bent them in unison.

Pastor Wallen smiled, "Let's join hands." He grabbed first Annie's hand on his right and then Chris' hand on his left. Bowing his head, he began to pray.

"Heavenly Father, there is a need present here today, please stand in the midst of us as we discuss it and let your purpose be revealed, Amen".

As he closed the prayer, Pastor Wallen looked up, his eyes opening wide in surprise!

The Beloved's had a tongue of fire right in the middle of each of their foreheads!

"What the hay!" he exclaimed as he stood quickly, knocking his chair over as he backed away, and tumbling to the ground. The Beloveds stood to their feet shocked. All of them puzzled by what had caused the pastor to react so violently. Ms. Wedner reappeared just then carrying a tray with coffee, milk and cookies.

"Oh my, my, my" Ms. Wedner sat the tray down and hobbled over to the pastor before the Beloved's could reach for him. "What's happened?" her confusion was apparent as she bent slowly to help him.

Ms. Wedner struggled to help the pastor to his feet, and gave a little cry of shocked outrage when he pushed her slightly to the side. He immediately grabbed Chris who was closest to him by both his arms and stared fixedly at his forehead.

"Pastor Wallen?" Chris blurted with a question and not a little fear in his voice.

The Pastor looked down, and noticing he was gripping Chris tightly, let go quickly and stepped back. "I'm so sorry Chris, I...I...looked up and you all had flames, no no, tongues of flame glowing on your foreheads! In all my years of pastoring I've never seen anything like it!"

The Beloved's looked at each other, or rather at each other's foreheads and saw nothing out of the ordinary. John, afraid that this might alter Pastor Wallen's plan to help began to explain.

"Pastor, you've had a small glimpse of what our family has been experiencing over the last three days." His voice was desperate and he could hear it, but continued, "Please allow me to share our story. I believe the Lord has led us to you for a purpose." The pastor grabbed his chair, turned it upright and sat down heavily in response.

John proceeded to give a detailed accounting of the "family vacation" to this point, including the older gentleman at the casino, Chris and Sara's accident, the shimmering in the salt flats, and the incident at the campground. When he was finished, John folded his hands in the steeple he'd been taught to use for his prayers, set his lips on them and stared at Pastor Wallen who had begun to sweat profusely. No one noticed Ms. Wedner quietly sliding down the wall and fainting dead away...

***

Pastor Wallen had heard many confessions in his lifetime, but he had to admit he was stumped. This was like a confession in reverse. He looked toward Lois to gauge her reaction and was the first to notice her collapsed on the floor.

He stood abruptly and took four long strides to her side. "Lois, Lois", the concern in his voice was accompanied by his hand softly patting her cheek.

Ms. Wedner made a low moaning sound and began to come around. Her eyelids fluttered open and she looked around the room.

"I'm so sorry, I...I.., it's been such a long time since I've experienced those flaming tongues, it just startled me, I am so sorry."   Pastor Wallen's look of astonishment told the Beloved's that he had no idea what his secretary was talking about.

Sara voice in the corner drew the attention of everyone in the room. "I believe we've found who we've been led to."   All eyes turned to Sara. The bright tongue of flame glowed like a star from the middle of her forehead.

Outside of Time

Lucifer himself was involved in the progress of the Beloved family. Those in these circles know that a full out assault is imminent; the last two attempts, having failed miserably for those involved, left a continuous wail as background music. Payment for the second failed attempt.

Now the VG swine made it to the first of their five contacts. This increased their chances of success, which meant that if they were not destroyed and soon, this particular strategy would or could be delayed by several years inside time. Unacceptable! Unacceptable!

In a completely uncharacteristic move, Sara slowly approached Ms. Wedner crouched down and hugged her. Ms. Wedner seemed a little surprised, but hugged Sara back instinctively.

Sara pulled away slowly and looked into Ms. Wedner's eyes.

"I'm afraid Ms. Wedner; do you know what is going on here?"

Ms. Wedner nodded her head in the affirmative, and then shook it slowly back and forth creating varying degrees of confusion on the faces of each of the occupants in the room.

"Please child, Ms. Wedner said in her papery voice, help me to my feet"

Sara looked at her mom, who nodded her head, and Sara gently helped Ms. Wedner to her feet.

The elderly woman waivered a little but righted herself before turning to the group.

"I'm afraid this is going to be a rather long story. Ms. Wedner's smile was shaky. "I guess I always knew that this would come around to me again. I just wish I was a little younger. Here her eyes misted just a little with sorrow and memories.

Pastor Wallen put a reassuring arm around his long-time secretary's shoulder, though whether for himself or her he was not sure. As he held his long-time friend steady on her feet, she appeared like a small child, but he felt the strength straighten her spine as she looked at each of the four Beloveds in turn, stopping and smiling brightly when her eyes moved to Sara.

"I remember being your age darling girl". She began wistfully, "what are you sixteen…seventeen?"

"Fifteen ma'am" Sara's reply was respectful but tinged with confusion.

Still smiling brightly, Lois continued, "the fear, the excitement, the desire, and that itching you get right before you do something you know is wrong…do you know what I'm talking about Sara?"

Sara smiled brightly knowing she'd found a new friend for life and tentatively nodded "yes".

Ms. Wedner shrugged off the pastor's steadying hand and walking over to Sara grabbed her hands. The remaining three Beloved's and Pastor Wallen stared mesmerized at this interplay between wisdom and youth.

"I was like you once Sara Beloved. I believed my purpose was about me, and I believed that if I wanted something, my purpose was to claim it!" She emphasized her statement by squeezing Sara's hand, "Do you ever feel that way Sara?"

Sara seemed completely hypnotized by Ms. Wedner's calming voice and spoke without hesitation, "I feel that way a lot of the time." A small nervous laugh accompanied her confession, and Ms. Wedner giggled like a girl.

"Yes, I remember." Lois Wedner's voice became distant and quiet as she began to tell a story that would change the course of every life in the room.

June 25, 1947 New Mexico

In her sixteenth year, Lois Cantor was a beautiful young woman. She lived, quite happily, in Santa Fe, New Mexico on her paternal grandparents' farm.

Her only remaining parent, her father, had been killed a year earlier; not in the war, but driving home drunk one evening, when he lost control of his car and ran it into a ditch. Officer Buley had driven out to give her grandparents the news.

She remembered vividly the hushed explanations, her grandmother's cry of grief as she fell to her knees, and her grandfather's stoic resolve as he gently pulled her Grammy upright again. Lois watched silently from the stairs, letting her tears of loss fall as she remembered her father's sober smiles and drunken mournful stares.

It had been devastating, but not surprising to Lois. Her father had not been the same without her mother, who had died three years earlier; taken by cancer. Her grandparents were all she had now. There were a smattering of distant relatives, but she knew she would always have a home with her Nan and Pops.

Lois was petite and slender, with lovely natural blonde hair that curled in wisps around her forehead, flowing golden down her back. Her eyes sparkled like blue aquamarines (at least that's what one of her beaux had told her).

On this particular morning, Lois had woken bathed as much in excitement as she was in the sunlight streaming into her bedroom from the window. She dressed quickly ready to go see what preparations had been made for her grand party.

Her grandmother Betty hugged her when she entered the kitchen for breakfast, kissing her forehead and singing happy birthday in her ear.

Lois knew that she was lucky to have her grandparents. They were good Christian folk and provided a good home with lots of love.

She could often become difficult and bitter as she struggled with the grief of her loss and the loneliness of being an orphan. She knew this was when her grandparents prayed for her most. They sensed, she believed, how easy it would be for her to just drift away into the same empty relief her father had succumbed to. The world outside was changing so fast, and their own fears kept Lois close to home.

But today was different...special. Lois had determined before she'd left her room that today she would not be depressed. She was going to have the best sweet sixteen party in the county! A barn burner that would in fact take place in her grandparents' barn!

There would be a big band and food and a new dress that shimmered like water, blue and silken with small white rose buds at the corners of her sleeves.

Lois could hardly contain herself when she stepped back from her grandmother's embrace and looked around the kitchen. Every inch of counter space was taken up with her Nan's baking and cooking. Her smile glowed as she asked how she could help.

Nan just smiled at her with careworn eyes. "You go over to the Harkers' and ask Emily if we can borrow that pretty cut glass punch bowl set she likes to show off at church. I've got everything under control here".

Lois smiled back at her grandmother before blowing her a kiss and breezing out the kitchen door to take the trail through the brush that led to Mrs. Emily Harker's home. Lois could hear Nan yelling out the door "not to dawdle".

Lois laughed and picked a lonely cornflower as she walked, twirling it in the light breeze that lifted her hair from her shoulders. "What kind of word is dawdle…hee hee, such a silly word."

Her mind was feeling lazy and subdued, when suddenly it popped into Lois' head that her grandmother was sad, and needed prayer. This was followed just as quickly by a second thought, "I'll do it when I get home." and that was that.

She looked up to see the tree line ahead that separated her grandparent's farm from the Harker's.   It was still half a mile away and she let her mind drift as she walked. "Would Jim Juarez ask her to dance?   Would Liam Drake be jealous if he did?" questions and scenarios ran through her mind as if she had lived her sixteenth birthday already and was just waiting to catch up to it.

But just as a negative thought slashes through a happy mind, Lois' happy revelry was interrupted. Just as she reached the line of the trees, a brilliant flash slashed through the sky…

His Loving Word Church, NE 1:45 pm

Lois regained herself and was staring at the Beloved's again. Her fear had been growing as the memories came flooding back. She looked at each of the Beloved's, saving Sara for last. She knew in this young girl she'd found what she liked to call a 'Soul Sister'. Lois knew jive talk, she'd learned so much in her travels with Carl. In this instance, the meaning was totally different and yet totally the same.   Lois connected with Sara. She'd known when she asked Sara about feeling alone, that Sara would understand.

It had long been Lois' contention (and she'd been contentious with the Pastor about it) that the Lord had created just a few "types" of personalities, and that each individual's 'soul' made the personality unique to them. She could see that she and Sara were 'cut from the same cloth'.

As she stared at her new friend, Lois could still see the bright orangish-yellow flame, glowing like a bright tongue on Sara's forehead. She reached out and patted Sara's hand.

"Sara, what I am about to share with you all will be frightening". At this Sara pulled her hand back and tears formed in her eyes. "Shh, shh, there now honey" wisdom and understanding were shining from her eyes as she held tightly to Sara's hand which continued trying to pull free.

"I was afraid like you. And I wish I could say I overcame it, but that would be a lie." This was said as Lois reached her free hand up, hesitantly pulling it back two or three times as if she were fearful of touching something hot, before finally laying her soft wrinkled hand to the flame on the young girl's forehead.

As she did, fingers bent by time and arthritis, straightened miraculously. To a one, the jaws of everyone in the room unhinged.

Lois flexed her healed hand in front of her face laughing quietly, and continued speaking, unaffected by the slack jaws.

"But I know the power of this light…this flame…and once you do, it sure helps keep the fear at bay."

Sara seemed to relax completely, just as blown away by what she'd witnessed as she was by how calm her spirit had become at Lois' words.

"Now, where was I?" Lois questioned absently, holding tightly to Sara's hand, "Oh yes, yes now I remember, the flash…"

June 25, New Mexico 1947

Lois' piercing scream more than likely split the air, but no one heard it.

A loud shimmering pop seemed to be ripping the fabric of the sky wide open before Lois' eyes.

It almost looked to Lois, who was by this time cowering behind the trees, as if a piece of parchment with a fire lit in the middle was burning a whole outward, but instead of fire, electricity burned the edges of the sky back. Lois began hyperventilating; terror making it hard to breath.

Was the Lord coming back? If so, why was He coming through New Mexico? She knew even as she thought it, that it could not be right. Her grandmother had told her that in the second coming…

Lois stopped breathing all together as a disc shaped aircraft boomed through the hole in the parchment sky and streaked across the horizon. She turned to see it flying directly over her grandparents farm when a more earthly explosion seemed to rock the aircraft and several large pieces jettisoned off and crashed… into her HOME!

Lois turned without hesitation and began running back toward her home, her grandparents, and the fire that now engulfed both the house and barn…

His Loving Word Church, NE 2:15 pm

Lois paused in her story once more and drew the breath she'd been unable to when it had actually happened.   Then she looked at Sara once again.

Tears watered Lois' blue eyes, and Sara reached up and gently wiped them away, then quite unexpectedly began to cry herself.

"They died didn't they?" There was such heartbreak in Sara's voice, that all Lois could do was pull her in close and hug her tightly. As she did her head nodded furiously in the affirmative.

"Yes, they did." Lois used the sleeve of her dress to wipe her eyes as she pulled back from Sara.   Then, to Sara's surprise, a smile lit up Lois' face and where once there was sorrow, now shown great joy.   "However, as always when you belong to the Lord, great good also came out of it."

New Mexico June 25, 1947

Lois reached the back door to the kitchen screaming her grandmother's name, and begging God in her mind to spare her Nan.

Black smoke poured out of the kitchen door and Lois was choking and retching before she even reached it.

An explosion rocked the house as the gas line from the stove was absorbed by the greedy flames and Lois was thrown backward twenty feet from the door. She landed in a twisted heap near a tree where a tire swing hung.

Through the shockwaves pulsing through her brain, she flashed to the memory of coming home from school to find the swing there, a present from her grandfather. Her grandfather! He was in the barn!

Lois desperately tried to push herself up to run to her grandfather's aid, but her arms puddled like jelly beneath her. She looked first at the right which was twisted completely around so that she was looking at the back of her hand when it should have been her palm.

Fighting for clarity, her head swam dizzily as she glanced at her left arm and saw some type of white sharp object protruding from shoulder. It took her three blinks of her eyes…she remembered counting them… to realize it was bone torn through the skin. Her stomach swam nauseously as she looked around to see if anyone had heard the explosion and was coming to help. Her last conscious thought was "are those sirens or warning bells?"

His Loving Word Church, NE 2:40 pm
Lois looked small and exhausted when she paused this time. Pastor Wedner, who'd never been aware of any of the revelations Lois was now sharing, sat spellbound with the Beloveds.

When Lois spoke it was quietly, shakily, "I haven't repeated these things for over thirty years. I had no idea how memories could wear a person out."

John, who'd been mesmerized by the picture being painted, stood quickly at her words, pulling his wife up with him. He felt they were hurting this poor woman rather than finding answers to their own dilemma.

"Ms. Wedner", he stuttered, but stopped abruptly, when Ms. Wedner politely held up her hand as if to ask a question.

"Please, call me Lois."

John smiled and nodded, acknowledging her request. "Please Lois, we don't want to cause any harm or hurt to you. You've been more than generous with your"…

Before he could finish Lois stood herself. She looked at each of them individually, and smiling, let her Christ shine through.

A brilliance, there was no other way to explain it, lit the small office as if the Sun had been lassoed and let loose within its walls. White perfect light, radiating not with heat, but with life, pulsed through each of them. Like dominoes they fell to their knees or backs in quick succession speaking in the spirit and praising God.

When five or so minutes had passed, each occupant of the room opened their eyes and looked around at each other in wondrous confusion and then at Lois.

The diminutive woman of everyone's focus was seated again and gazing at each of them with such blessed assurance that Pastor Wallen and the Beloveds were tempted to kneel at her feet so that she could minister to them the word of the Lord. As if she sensed it, Lois spread her arm in the direction of the other chairs around her inviting everyone to sit again.

Once each of them had settled in their respective seats, wiping their eyes or grinning from ear to ear, Lois began to speak again.

New Mexico June 25 1947

Darkness.

Darkness covered her at times like a warm blanket and at others like a prison.

Lois was completely "unaware" most of the first week that she lay in a coma from the head trauma she'd sustained when landing near the tree.

When there was awareness, all she could register was pain. It crept through her spine, down her arms, and through her head like a giant spider, causing her to shift in the darkness as she tried to escape its web.

During these attempted escapes she could hear murmurings and then a slight burning in her leg, as if the spider, tired of her struggles, had bitten her. Then the darkness would swallow her again.

As her body began to heal and Lois began to retreat from the dark, she began to have conscious thought. Her first was of lying in a bed.

"Was she home? Had she been sick and missed her own birthday party?" Her reason however remained fuzzy and she would have nightmares of her grandparents standing in flames holding their arms out to her, begging for her help, or they were driving away in the truck her grandfather kept running with hangars and ladies pantyhose.

Only they wouldn't look back. They wouldn't wave. They wouldn't say goodbye.

Alone and afraid, she would cringe in her mind as shadows with sharp teeth crept in from the corners of the darkness to accuse her. "You killed them you selfish girl! You let them die, burned to death!" Her struggles to escape the accusations always resulted in another spider bite, "but at least" her mind would argue, "it brought peace."

On a Friday, two weeks after her grandparent's home exploded in fire, Lois opened her eyes.

She looked around the room with blurry eyes searching for the dandelion calendar that hung on the wall in her room, but nothing was familiar.   Her first attempt to call out for her grandmother came out as small as a mouse's squeak. Looking around dizzily, she cleared her throat and tried again.

Just then, a large squat Hispanic woman in a nurse's uniform, walked up to her bed and seeing Lois' eyes open threw her arms wide shouting. "Baby girl, baby girl you're awake!"

Lois was so startled by this greeting that tears watered the corners of her eyes.

"Who was this woman? Had something happened? Where were her grandparents?" Then, like a swollen river her eyes spilled over as memories came rushing back.   Fragmented and shadowed by fear, she remembered; the shimmering, the explosion!

She looked up at the nurse who was holding tightly to the rails of her bed. Tears ran rivulets down the stranger's face and Lois asked in a voice squeaky with loss and heartbreak, "Where are they? Where are my grandparents?"   The nurse, whose name was Angela Vasquez, smiled at the small young woman lying on the bed.

"How was anyone going to let this little girl know what had happened?" Angela wondered.

She was officially an orphan. No trace of family except an aunt of Lois' now deceased grandmother, had been found.   A great, great Aunt, well into in her eighties, and unable to care for someone Lois' age.

Angela sat gently on the edge of the bed. She knew that Lois, having been in a coma for two weeks, had not yet fully experienced the pain from her injuries, but she knew it would come. She had worked in critical care nursing since the beginning of the war, mostly to be there and pray for those whose lives were coming to an end. Sometimes however, through God's mercy, she was able to pray with a patient instead of over them.

No one who'd been there the day Lois was brought in had believed she would actually live. Both her arms had suffered severe trauma. The compound fracture in her left arm was the worst, and infection had set in on the second day. The shock that set in immediately after the accident had left Lois' body too weak to fight and for five days, the fever that possessed her fought to kill her. There was a point when her attending physician, Dr. Iowa, had seriously considered removing her arm to save her life, but Angela had asked for one more day to pray.

She and Dr. Iowa were good friends; in fact it could be argued they were related, since their families were from the same reservation. They both attended the same revival that led to both of them accepting Christ which made it possible for them to go to the Lord agreeing together in situations like this. Sometimes the Lord said yes, and sometimes He said no. Regarding Lois' arm, He said yes!

"Well", Angela remembered thinking at the time, "the Lord has a plan for you little one". Since then, she'd diligently prayed; often right beside Lois' bed. She'd felt led to seek God's intervention and had encouraged others to pray for her as well. "Lois", she'd speak softly to the unconscious girl, "You will be o.k.! We will storm the gates of heaven with our prayers."

Now she stared into her charge's lovely sad eyes. "I am so blessed to see you awake honey. I'm gonna go get the doctor o.k.?"

Lois clutched desperately at the nurse. Her words were croaky and soft as she asked, "My grandparents?"

Angela squeezed her hand back. "I'm gonna let the doctor talk to you first and then we'll talk about your grandparents o.k.?"

Lois nodded her head yes, as her tears slipped from her grasp much as her consciousness had over the last few weeks. She knew that if her grandparents were alive and alright nothing would keep them from being here with her and their absence frightened her.   She turned her head and watched as a breeze blew the petals on the rose bushes just outside her window back and forth lazily.

"Lord", her mind quietly implored, "I really don't understand. I am not sure why you left me all alone, or why my grandparents aren't here, or why you even let me live. Please help me understand".

Before the she could finish her plea, she heard a still small voice speak, as if someone had taken the nurse's place at the edge of her bed.

"I will never leave you nor forsake you, trust in me."

Lois was not especially comforted, but she knew that for the first time in her life the LORD GOD JEHOVAH had determined to speak to her. Just when she would have continued the conversation, Nurse Vasquez walked in with a short, moon-faced man sporting a black braid that fell to the middle of his back.

"Well, look whose back." His jovial manner and kind eyes, gave Lois hope. "How are you feeling?"

Croak "o.k., Where are my grandparents?"

Nurse Vasquez had come around the other side of the bed and brushed the fingertips of Lois' damaged left arm. The Doctor, whose name was Laughing Bird, although he went by Dr. Iowa, was a middle-aged man with a warm smile. He sat on the edge of her bed and looked compassionately into Lois' eyes. Then he tore the band aid off.

"Honey, your grandparents didn't make it."

And even though she'd known it, and even though she thought she was prepared to deal with it, Lois began to wail from the pit of her heart. The pain of her loss was so deep it immediately overwhelmed her and she dropped unwillingly back into unconsciousness.

Angela looked up at the doctor who was stroking Lois' hair and mumbling quietly. "Dr., what are you doing?"

"Praying to my Lord and Savior Jesus Christ, Angie" Dr. Iowa smirked,

Angela became flustered by the doctors nodding look and released Lois' fingertips before moving back around to the other side of the bed.

"Well, I'm thinking that since this poor little girl, who lost her grandparents ON HER SIXTEENTH BIRTHDAY, is now an orphan I might just see if she wants to come stay with me awhile!" There let him stick that in his pipe and smoke it!

The doctor held back a chuckle as he replied, "I think that would be lovely Angie. I was just wondering if I was going to have to tell my wife that we were going to have to raise another child." Angela began to giggle like a girl. She knew that Dr. Iowa and his wife had raised and shooed seven children from the nest. Now that conversation would have been worth seeing.

"Well, let's give her some rest. There will be plenty of time to work on the details after she's had time to deal with all this." Dr. Iowa turned to leave the room, but glanced back at Lois before catching Angela's eye.

She saw the pain as he spoke. "I know that all things work to the good for them that love the Lord and are the called according to His purpose, but danged if this one makes any sense to me." He gave a small shrug before walking from the room.

Angela resumed her vigil beside Lois' bed, and lightly brushed her forehead, praying all the while.

Lois stood at the back door looking through the screen at her grandmother who was smiling and repeating "Don't you dawdle...don't you dawdle".

Lois turned to go to Ms. Harker's and get the cut-glass punch bowl set when flames erupted in front of her forming a half circle. She turned to run back to her grandmother, but her grandmother stood behind the screen engulfed in fire.

Staring wide-eyed at her granddaughter she raised her arm and pointed a finger that shown white at the tip where the flesh had burned away, "...And strangers shall stand and feed your flocks, and the sons of aliens shall be your plowmen and your vinedressers...", then Lois' grandmother slowly retreated into the flames, her scorched smile mimicking hilarity.

Lois began to scream and beg her grandmother to come out, come out where it was safe, but Nan quietly disappeared into the darkness.

Lois followed her into the void.

The Loving Word Church, NE 3:00 pm

The tension in Pastor Wedner's office was palpable. Each member of the Beloved family (except for Sara) sat forward in their chairs; anxiety and anticipation in their posture.

Sara sat next to Lois holding her hand and listening intently, when suddenly the small, frail, beautiful Lois jumped to her feet as if she were a child who'd been told it was playtime.

She looked quickly at each face in the room, "How bout we go to my house and I'll fix us all a nice dinner and we can continue our conversation." At her words, John stood too, waving his hands in supplication,

"We really don't want to take up too much more of your time Ms. Wedner…a nod…Pastor."

We have to be in Virginia in six more days, and I'm sorry, (this apologetically as he looked at Ms. Wedner) but I'm not sure if your story is helping us get closer to what's going on here."

Lois did not appear upset or disappointed, she simply sidled over to John and grabbing his face between her hands kissed him on the top of the forehead. His eyelids fluttered suddenly and he began to fall to the ground, speaking words unfamiliar to anyone in the room.

Annie let out an "Oh" and scrambled to help John from the floor, but Lois touched her gently on the arm and told her matter-of-factly "Oh, he's just slain in the spirit; he'll get up when the Lord's done talking to him." She looked at the gathered group with a spark in her eyes and asked once more "Now who's up for dinner?" In unison the group's hands shot up, and they each took a half step back from the little powerhouse in their midst.

"Great!" If there was such a thing as a twinkle in an eye, she owned it as she walked with the vigor of a twenty year old toward the door to the pastor's office. She called back over her shoulder "Pastor, I'm going home to make chicken and dumplings for dinner. You bring the Beloved's along with you. I want them to see the farm."

The three Beloved's not slain in the spirit and Pastor Wallen were left staring at each other like mental patients in a psych ward, slack jaws and all. Finally Annie shook her head and bent to help her husband from the floor.

"John, honey, you o.k.?" She grabbed his hand to help him up, and was instantly slain in the spirit next to her husband. Sara, Chris, and Pastor Wallen watched this with equal surprise to John's own slaying and each took a synchronized step back again when Chris, in his usual easy manner quipped, "Um, let's just wait for them to come around like Ms. Wedner suggested."

Chapter 8

Nebraska, 2001 – Wedner Farm

Lois hummed 'Our God is an Awesome God' as she worked on her grandma's chicken and dumplings recipe. The cooked carrots and a peach cobbler stewed and bubbled.

She looked out over the sink that faced the front yard of her three acre farm and smiled at the tire swing that hung from a mature Cedar in her front yard.   Lois knew the T.V. psychiatrist she watched from time to time would probably have a field day with Lois and her house.   It was not an exact replica of her grandparent's farm, but it was close. Down to the white fence that had separated her grandparents farm from their neighbors the Harkens.

Since almost no one left alive knew about the tragedy that had befallen her on her sixteenth birthday, she rarely worried about what others thought. Now however, with the Beloved's and the pastor coming for dinner, the similarities were going to be readily apparent from the moment they turned into the drive.

Drudging   up   the   memories,   the adventures…and the loss; both excited her and brought back the fear of knowing. It had been so long since she'd even allowed the memories to come to her consciousness, she wasn't even sure if she could finish her story!

As quickly as this last thought penetrated her mind however, the spirit descended on her and she prayed in a tongue she did not know and went back to work on dinner.

The Beloved's followed Pastor Wallen in his beat up powder blue Ford pickup as he wended over the plains towards Lois's farm. The SUV was very quiet, each Beloved lost in thoughts of how the day was unfolding so far.

John finally spoke up, "So, is everyone still 'in this til the end'?" Laughter erupted in the SUV. It was family laughter, the most special and healing kind. The kind of laughter you can share with people who know you and love you anyway. The kind of laughter that leaves you breathless, or ready to pee your pants, or causes tears to stream down your eyes; which happened to each of them in varying degrees before the laughter caught in their throats at the sight of Lois' farm.

"It's like a painting", Sara shared breathlessly.

The azure sky was bright with wonderful pink and gold tones and the long shadows of the day fell on the perfect A-frame two-story home with red shutters. White washed and glowing in the dying light of the day, it was magical as the animals lowed or neighed at their arrival.

Chris pointed out the huge cedar that canopied the front of the house and shadowed the window where Lois waved to each of them from the kitchen. A tire swing hung low to the ground, and with the magic that belongs only to a tire swing, drew seventeen year old Chris and fifteen year old Sara immediately to it.

John and Annie left them in the yard and continued with Pastor Wallen up the wrap around veranda porch to the front door. The pastor rapped twice on the wood screen door and opened it as Lois appeared. She greeted them with a wide smile as she dusted her flour-covered hands on an old fashioned fifties era apron with pretty little yellow daisies pollenating the front.

"Welcome, welcome and shalom!" Lois laughed as they entered. "Follow me, I've got a nice glass of wine for each of you and some assorted cheeses." The floor boards creaked as she led them towards the dining room, "Carl – that's my late husband- and I used to love to have wine and cheese before dinner".

Lois paused suddenly and wiped a tear that had fallen quite by accident. "We'd laugh and he'd say 'Is your wine to your liking Ms. Hoity-Toity?' and I'd reply 'Why yes Mr. Hoity-Toity, its lovely'. It was our private joke being such simple country folk and all." Another tear escaped its confine but was easily captured by her knowing hands.

Chris, by this time, had come in from the yard. Ever the charmer he walked over to Lois and put a familiar arm around her while replying, "Ms. Wedner, I don't think you'll convince anyone in this room that you are 'simple country folk.'" Laughter slipped from their lips and Lois' tears were dried with a girlish giggle.

The screen door slammed sharply and everyone turned to see Sara walk in the house.

"Ms. Wedner, is it just me, or is this house exactly like the one you described that belonged to your grandparents?"

Lois' eyes squinted in consideration of her answer, "Sara is sharp Lord", she thought, "she was the only one to comment on the connection, I can see why you picked her." She turned to her new friend, "Actually Sara, you are very observant, and yes this is very similar to the farm I grew up on, with a few purposeful exceptions." All eyes turned to Lois as she spoke and she could see their confusion; except for Sara who just smiled broadly as she looked around the home.

"Well, since I have everyone's attention, and everyone's here, let's eat and I will continue my story." There was mystery in the air as she led them into a large enclosed dining room. The walls were all a light pine that lit up the room. A lovely floor to ceiling hutch, made of the same wood, was set in the wall. Delicate china dishes with very similar daisies to those dusting Lois' apron were lovingly placed on each of the hutch's shelves. A large pine table took up the rest of the room. It seated ten, but with such a small group, Lois had only set the head of the table and two chairs to the left and three on the right, but what a setting!

The Beloved family gasped one breath at the beauty of the table and room.

The china from the pine hutch graced the table with amber goblets and gold plated utensils. Two large vases contained wild-flowers with daisies in the center of each, and a chandelier that looked to be authentic Tiffany created a rainbow reflection in the pine turning the room into a kaleidoscope of color.

"It's like being in heaven." Sara's comment was hushed as if she'd entered a chapel. Lois was quick to respond. "Carl and I felt a little closer to the Lord when we had dinner here." she smiled remembering, "It feels a little like eating in the throne room of the Lord, doesn't it?"

Sara could only nod, and watch as the Tiffany glass created dappling drops of rainbow beauty around her. Lois leaned in and whispered in her ear, "I knew you'd like it Sara." before turning back to the group at large and spreading her hands wide.

"Pastor, you're at you're usual spot at the head of the table. I'll sit on your right so I can see our guests."

With these instructions the Beloved's scrambled to sit. The smells coming from the kitchen could only be described as 'blessed'. Lois walked through the swinging door near the hutch to get back to the kitchen. Sara noticing her father and the Pastor locked in discussion looked to her mother, but she was busy brushing Chris' hair out of his eyes and wiping dust from his face.

"If she looks my way, I'm next."

She stood abruptly causing her chair to scrape and all conversation to cease as everyone looked at her expectantly. "I-I- I'm just going to go see if Ms. Wedner needs any help." This seemed to be a great relief to everyone and Sara almost burst out laughing. "What? Did they think I was going to slay them in the spirit or something?" She laughed to herself as she walked through the swinging door Lois had disappeared into.

Lois turned to see Sara enter the kitchen and smiled at her expectantly. "I was just wondering if you might want some help Ms. Wedner." Lois turned and dusted her hands, more out of habit than needing to clean them.

"Well, Ms. Sara you are just in time, if you'll grab the carrots and biscuits I'll bring the chicken and dumplings and the relish tray." They met at the butcher block loaded with food in the middle of the kitchen and Lois handed Sara her items to carry before picking up the rest.

They swung through the door leading to the dining room and were greeted by ooh's and ahh's as everyone finished the cheese and crackers they'd been munching on.

"Well, I hope this is to everyone's liking." Lois beamed as she took her seat.

As anxious to eat as he was to hear the rest of Lois' story, Pastor Wallen grabbed his secretary's hand as soon as she sat, and Sara's who had the seat on his left. "Let's go to the Lord in prayer."

***

Lois could not remember the last time she had had so much fun at dinner. The Beloved's truly were a wonderful family and their love and affection for each other was readily apparent.

"Wouldn't it be wonderful?" she thought "If I could…no no no, never mind Lord."

Before she could revisit the idea growing like a germ in her mind, Annie looked at her and quietly asked "Ms. Wedner, do you feel like continuing your story?" Before Lois could form a reply John spoke up.

"Um, listen, I know that we are here at the Lord's request." A smile rode across his lips, "But I don't know if this is our destination, or if we need to get out of here and get to the Shroud." He stopped and looked into Lois' eyes before continuing, "Is your story going to help us determine that?" Lois sensed his fear and grabbed his hand before she replied, "Fear not, for I am with you, lo even til the end of the earth." John's expression turned quizzical at her quote from the scripture so she went on.

"I believe you are here right now exactly where you need to be, and when it is time to go, I believe the Lord will leave you with no doubt.

My story somehow, someway is intricately knit with your own. I believe you need to hear it."

Lois leaned back and watched John's reaction. "Oh he's a smart one he is."

His face took on the look of a man in deep thought, and then his eyes closed as if in prayer. He finally opened his eyes and looked at Lois, Pastor Wallen, and then his family.

"We stay." John shifted his eyes to Lois once again. "Please continue your story Ms. Wedner."

Lois smiled and looked at the room as a whole. Well, alright then! "Let's pray and I'll begin".

Chapter 9

New Mexico 1947

Lois was finally going home. After eight weeks in the hospital and painful almost unbearable physical therapy, she was finally being discharged from the hospital, but to where?

No one had really spoken about where she'd go or what exactly had happened at her grandparents' farm.

She had visited her Nan and Pops graves in a wheelchair and hospital clothes.

Everything she had (her pretty party dress included) had burned with the farm. All that was left were these stone markers, bleak and without life. She was bereft, alone, and lost.

Angela, her nurse and now good friend, anxious to cheer her up had shared the news that Lois was now a millionaire, right in front of their graves.

She told her how much her grandparents had loved her and cared about her wellbeing. How they'd owned their farm and had substantial savings and insurance of which she was the sole heir.

This seemed irrelevant that day when all she wanted was to hear their voices one more time, but as she waited now to leave the hospital, it brought her some peace.

"I won't have to worry about being homeless", she thought, slouched sadly in her wheelchair, "I just won't have anyone to share it with", and she began to cry deep racking sobs.

Angela was at her side before she'd heard her pull up. The nurse wrapped her arms around her and "tut tutted" to help quiet her favorite patient.

"Nina, don't cry baby". She said as she stroked her hair softly. "You will never be alone. You will always have a family who loves you."

Lois was so consumed by her grief she barely noticed that Angela had read her thoughts.

Lois flung her casted arms out knocking away Angela's arms, before pulling them back and wincing in pain.

"Who? What family do I have?!" the anguish in her voice was so hopeless, and came out gruff and mean-spirited.

Angela laughed. A small laugh mixed with an "Ahhh". A laugh that said "You don't know?"

She tilted Lois' head up with her fingers under her chin and looked her in the eyes.

"Why your Christian family of course, look across the street."

Lois turned her head in the direction Angela pointed to, her face reddened by her tears and sorrow.

Across the drive where cars and ambulances pulled up to the hospital stood a line of people, maybe fifty or sixty, stretching down the entrance to the hospital.

Some held signs with messages like "Get well soon", and "We love you Lois", some held candles, some flowers and Teddy Bears.

A huge cheer arose as she looked their way.

She recognized almost every one of them. Her grandparents' neighbors the Harkens were there, as was the pastor of her church. Even Jim Juarez and Liam Drake had come, both looking a bit embarrassed.

Quite beyond her control her hand rose to cover her mouth, but was stopped the crook of her elbow in the cast.

She rested her arm on the her lap as gratitude so deep it almost burst from her, caused her to shout at her new family, "THANK YOU!"

The crowd cheered again and started across the street towards her.

Lois, still reeling from her pain and loss began to panic, feeling that if they reached her she might surely dissolve into misery and disappear.

She turned to ask Angela to please get her in the car, but saw that Angela had seen her fear and was ahead of her as usual. Her friend started forward to meet the crowd and headed straight for the Pastor of their church.

"Pastor Jesse", she said loudly so that everyone would hear, "I think Lois should get home and to bed. Would you mind saying a prayer before we leave?"

Pastor Jesse small in stature and slight in build, was an astute and wise pastor who had been leading his small congregation for over eight years.

He realized when Angela approached them that she was concerned about her patient's mental state, so he turned to the crowd, and putting his hands up made a quieting motion, before addressing everyone.

"Lois is very tired everyone, and overcome by your support. Let's pray for her before she leaves, and then we can schedule visits with her bodyguard...laughs from the crowd...I mean nurse."

Angela gave him a grimacing smile before he continued, "Let's bow our heads."

As the crowd followed his request, Pastor Jesse began to pray.

"Dear Lord, most gracious God, continue to heal the hurts both physical and emotional of our sister Lois, give her your grace, peace, and mercy, in Christ's name, Amen."

The large crowd "Amen'd in agreement and began waving and blowing kisses as they left their gifts behind Angela's car and walked toward their vehicles or back to their homes.

Lois, who had sat and listened, kept her head down as she was helped into the vehicle. "Where do I go now Lord?"

Wedner Farm Nebraska, 2001

Lois looked around the table gauging each person's response. She stood and stretched then sat again.

"Well, I went to stay with Angela and her family and believe me it was a tight squeeze, but she became a second mother to me and I was very grateful, even if I didn't show it at the time." Lois had a faraway look as she continued.

"I never returned to school. I was very self-conscious about the scars on my arms and would get overwhelmed with…what is the term they use today…oh yes, I would get overwhelmed with panic attacks every time I left the front yard, but I was able to complete my high school diploma through correspondence."

"I went to church on Sunday's but I had become an introvert, letting the trauma of the event become a big ball of fear in my heart and mind."

"Unfortunately, I can't get into detail or we'd be here a week so I'm gonna skip forward a couple of years to when I came into my inheritance from my grandparents."

New Mexico, 1950

Lois wound her car slowly up the drive of her grandparents' farm.

Since she could not live there alone, Angela (who had become her legal guardian along with Pastor Jesse) had arranged for a lovely family to rent the property until Lois came of age or felt she was ready to move back in or sell it. About a month after her nineteenth birthday, she felt she was ready to move in and hire help to keep the farm going.

It had been rebuilt and looked exactly as it had before the tragedy. The tire swing on the tree had been replaced because the heat had melted it down into a rubber blob.

Lois took it all in at a glance and felt a little fear, some grief, but mostly joy. She was home. Putting the car in park, she got out and started up the walk to the kitchen door.

Mrs. Harken appeared at the door startling her. "Oh Lois, I am so glad you're here! Your grandmother would be so proud of you", all of this said as Mrs. Harken flew open the screen door and pulled Lois into her embrace.

Lois allowed herself to be hugged and gave a quick squeeze back before stepping away.

"Thank you Mrs. Harken, um was I supposed to meet you here?"

Mrs. Harken laughed at Lois trying to be polite about asking what she was doing there.

"No honey", I just wanted to make sure things were ready for your homecoming." Mrs. Harken smiled honestly and swept her arm into the kitchen so that Lois could step past her.

Lois' heart fluttered, just a little, as she stepped into her grandmother's… no that wasn't right… her kitchen.

She immediately felt home settle into her soul. "Oh how she'd missed this", she thought nostalgically.

It had been a miracle that she'd had Angela's family to help her through her grief, but she missed 'HOME', and now here she was.

She could see by looking around that Mrs. Harken had been cleaning, and the house looked wonderful.

Before she could turn to thank her, Mrs. Harken came and hugged her from behind. "You o.k. honey?" she asked quietly.

"I will be", Lois replied squeezing Mrs. Harken's arm around her shoulders. "I think I just need a little time to take all of this in."

"Angie said she'd come by tomorrow and help set up a routine" Sara said giggling, "You know how she loves her routines."

Mrs. Harken laughed behind her.

Angela was well known for keeping their pastor on task at the church; in love of course Angela would say, but she and the pastor had had more than one argument about her "spiritual gifts".

"Well", Mrs. Harken stated pulling away and quickly wiping a tear from her eye before Lois could see it, "I know you've got lots to do, and I'm sure Ray is going to be waiting for supper so I will leave you to your home."

She started to walk out the kitchen's screen door when Lois reached for her hand and squeezed it.

The older woman turned and watched two lonely tears run down Lois' face as she mouthed

"Thank you so much", before turning back toward her home.

Lois closed the screen and walked into the dining room choosing a chair at her grandmother's (no its mine now) lovely table and bowed her head,

"Lord, here I am. I'm going to find out what happened to my grandparents, and I hope that's alright."

Lois' faith had grown since her home had been destroyed.

Attending church with Angela and seeing the support from friends and church members had shown her how real God was.

He continued to talk to her in her spirit especially during the first months of her grieving. He would reach in and quiet her spirit and give a word of love, or faith, and yes sometimes admonition.

Today however, Lois was taken by surprise, because rather than God speaking to her spirit, a man-being filled with light, and at least eight feet tall appeared at her right hand.

Lois knew that this was an angel. The knowledge was innate and she fell prone to the floor from her chair as he spoke.

"Daughter of Man, be in peace. I come to tell you the Lord has heard your prayers and knows you." Lois couldn't move but sensed the Lord's 'peace that passes all understanding' engulf her as the angel continued.

"He has work to be done at your hand", the being said in a voice like gentle rain as his peace brushed her face. "It will be difficult, but another will help you and you two will be joined as one flesh."

"Look for the revival in Roswell", he commanded as the glory began to fade from the room.

Lois wanted to jump up and shout "Hallelujah!" and "Glory to God" over and over, but could not move.

Wedner Farm Nebraska, 2001

Lois paused briefly. She had just divulged to the Beloved's, and Pastor Wallen, a secret she had only shared with Angela, her own husband, and a preacher long ago.

She needed to gauge if her words were going to make them run from the crazy lady or if they would believe.

They all sat staring at her intensely, hoping she'd continue, needing her to continue and so she did.

New Mexico 1950

"Please tell me; who am I looking for?" These words pressed at Lois' consciousness and lips, but her throat could not speak.

The angel disappeared completely then; in a flash like lightning and a colorful shimmering. Lois' body became her own again and she was instantaneously able to move. She jumped up frightened and confused. Her head swiveled back and forth like a Lazy Susan caught in a tug of war. She walked around her dining room twice before regaining her bearings and running to a cupboard of her hutch to grab a piece of paper and a pencil to write down all that the angel had said.

"Revival in Roswell?" Her mind puzzled, "what like a tent revival?"

Lois immediately went to the phone and asked the operator to dial Angela's home.   Mabel Dingle, also known as Miss Nosey, responded with a "You o.k. out their Lois? You feelin' o.k.?"

"Yes, I'm fine Mabel, please just…"

"Cuz I know you went home today for the first time and that can be real scary for a young girl, you sure you don't want…"

Lois interrupted, impatience heavy in her voice "Mabel, Mabel, I'm fine, I just need to speak with Angela is all."

"O.k. honey", Mabel's disappointment clashed with Lois' impatience, "if you're sure, here's your connection, have a nice evening."   Lois listened to the ringing on the line until Angela's youngest son Ernesto picked up the phone with an "Ola."

"Ernie, its Lois honey, let me speak to Mama."

"Lois!" five year old exuberance screamed into the phone, "We miss you!"

"I miss you too honey, now let me talk to MAMA!"   Her 'big sister' voice kicked in giving just the right amount of irritation. Suddenly in the background, the sound of the phone being yanked unwillingly from Ernesto's hand could be heard as Angela spoke, "Hello, hello?"

Lois, knowing that Mabel was more than likely listening through the line remained calm. "Mama, I know it is late, but is there any way you can come over tonight? I can't find my umm…umm…nightshirt. I thought I packed it but it is not here anywhere and you know I can't sleep without it." It took Angela a minute to respond and Lois could almost see the look of bewilderment on Angela's face before she replied.

"Oh yes, yes! Your nightshirt; I have it Nina, I'll bring it over after I get the babies to bed o.k.?"

"Perfect", Lois grinned, "Thank you Mama."

"O.k., baby." was followed by a click.

Lois spun to hang up the phone but not before whispering, "Good night Mabel."

Mabel, who'd been taking notes about no sleep and nightshirts, was caught unawares and whispered back, "Good night" before realizing she'd been found out and hanging up.

An hour later Lois watched as Papa Gus' pride and joy, his new Chevrolet truck, came winding up the drive. Angela jumped out and walked swiftly toward the door, opened it, stepped inside, turned around locked the door and then turned back to Lois.

"What is it baby, what's the matter?"

Suddenly, Lois didn't know where to begin. Angela had become so much to her. The thought of sharing what had happened and seeing any kind of doubt or derision on her face scared Lois. But her spirit spoke louder than her doubt and the conviction of what she saw would not allow her to be quiet for fear of ridicule. Before she knew what she intended to say she blurted, "An angel visited me tonight!"

Of all of the responses she expected; disbelief, hilarity, outrage, Angela's quiet calm and reverent fear were even more disconcerting. Lois opened her mouth intent on relaying all the being had told her, but Mama Angel held up a hand to silence her.

Angela stared enquiringly at Lois for some time before finally taking her gently by the hand

and leading her to the dining room table. She insisted Lois sit before she'd say a word. Lois complied more out of frustration at Mama Angel's silence than anything. When Angela took her time settling herself next to her adopted daughter, Lois was ready to scream!

After what seemed an eternity of prepping herself, Angela took a deep breath, said a silent prayer and finally opened her mouth. "I was hoping you would have more time sweet sister, I fear tribulation is at hand. Her face was full of sorrow and she kept a telling tempo by patting Lois' hand comfortingly.

"Before you tell me what the angel said, let me share the dream I've had since you came into our lives. I didn't want to share it with you until I knew it was time, and apparently the time has come. Prepare your heart Lois; the Lord has a purpose for you."

Lois listened to Angela's speech, and it was like hearing a stranger. In the three years since she'd come to know and love Angela, this was the first time Mama Angel had spoken to her so cryptically. Angela's love and kindness had helped Lois to heal, so what was this about preparing her heart and a dream?

"Mama, you're scaring me a little, and I am already terrified!" Lois almost shouted, and tried to stand from the table, but Angela kept her seated with the pressure on her hand.

"Baby girl, I'm not trying to scare you, but you have to know these things and begin to walk your path. Listen to what I have to tell you and then we are going to work on how to get you going, o.k.?"

Lois nodded in agreement holding tight to Angie's strength for support. Angela brushed

Lois' golden hair back from her beautiful lonely face and began to speak. "When you came into the hospital and were burnt and broken all I could think was 'have mercy Lord', but He spoke right back to me! Or maybe it was an angel, but I think it was the Lord." Angel gave her head a little shake, "It was definitely the Lord and He told me "Behold Mother, your daughter."

Tears filled Angela's eyes as she remembered the conversation. "Well, I wasn't exactly sure what the Lord was telling me yet, but I knew He was answering my prayer and being merciful to you." Lois listened intently, nodding her head so that Angela would continue. "So, I kissed you and prayed over you and went home that night and did what I do, you know, cook for Gus and the kids..." Angela's thoughts began to shift as she was transported to that night. She shook her head once again bringing herself back to the present.

"Anyway, that night I said my prayers and started to drift off to sleep when a man appeared at the side of my bed. He was about eight or nine feet tall and was as bright as a light bulb!" Angela had begun to perspire and she jumped up fanning herself. "I don't know if I'm having a hot flash, or the Spirit is setting me on fire!" She paused again to wipe her face and in between her bosom with a towel Lois had run to get from the bathroom.

"Can you go on now?" Lois wanted to know.

"Of course Niña, of course", Angela realized she had stopped at a very inopportune time in the story. "So, I see this man and I was very afraid, but I couldn't move or speak, and he says, Daughter of Man, peace, the Lord has seen your works and loves you.

Well I began in my head to praise His Holy Name, and this Being holds up his hand and I'm quieted! Then, and this is what you'll want to hear, he says, your daughter of the seed of forgiveness and light has a journey she must take without you. The Lord will provide for her, and her partner shall be he who is joined to her in the flesh." Angela moved around the room now as she talked before pausing to look lovingly at her 'Daughter of the seed and light'.

Awe and confusion warred on her face as she experienced once again being in the presence of one of the Lord's messengers. Who was she that the Lord was mindful of her? Or Lois for that matter? "I told Gus about 'the dream' and Pastor Jesse and they both said the same thing, "Don't tell her until the Lord tells you to."

Lois surprised Angela by bursting out laughing. It was such a strange moment in her life. She could not deny the eerily similar visitation Angela had experienced, but was struck instead by a picture of both their pastor and Papa Gus telling Mama Angel the same thing (and more than likely in the same tone) and her Mama's inevitable reaction, and she could not stop herself from laughing. Until she turned and noticed Mama's frown of hurt.

"Oh Mama, don't be upset. I'm at a loss as to what all of this means. The angel told me the same thing he told you, except he said look for the Revival in Roswell."

Angela whirled suddenly from her trek around the dining room, waving her arms while dancing in a circle and scaring Lois half out of her wits. What on earth had gotten into her Mama Angel?

Lois chased her for two revolutions around the table before catching her, looking her straight in the eyes and asking her, "What in the name of all that's holy are you doing?"

Angela felt glee wash over her like pure honey, thick and sweet. She basked in it for just a few seconds more before words would leave her.

"I received a letter today from our sister church in Roswell!" Angela's face split open in a grin that showed her lovely teeth, all of them. It was almost maniacal.   Tears streamed from her eyes and she found it very difficult not to lay on the floor and laugh, praising Jesus as she did, but she refrained for Lois' sake. "They are having a revival in two weeks!"

Lois reached unsteadily for the back of a dining room chair and grasped it with both hands as Angela shared the rest of her news. "They wanted us to post it so folks could invite their families to attend!"

Lois slowly sank to her knees and shook her head back and forth. "I'm not prepared for this." "I'm no one! I don't even teach a regular Sunday school class."

Angela came and kneeled beside her, "Let's pray Niña."

They both bowed their heads seeking reassurance as Angela led the prayer. "Lord, we are unworthy of your love or notice, but thank you for seeing us and please guide us now in your will, amen."

Angela looked up to see some of the fear erased from her baby's eyes. "Good", she thought, "Now we are ready to begin."

Chapter 10

Wedner Farm Nebraska, 2001

Lois' voice had grown horse. The sun had gone down long ago and shadows lurked outside the rainbow light that surrounded the table. She yawned noisily and smiled at each of them, but her eyes were drawn to the Beloved's young daughter. "Sara, I think that's enough for tonight, how about you?"

Sara briefly shook her head in the negative, wanting the story to continue, before respectfully changing direction and nodding a yes.

John and Annie smiled at their daughter, looked at each other, and then as only a well-oiled married couple could, prepared to exit quickly and graciously.

"Ms. Wedner, we appreciate all you've done for us." John's standard beginning sentence seemed to have lost some of its sincerity. "But we really have to be on the road first thing in the morning. Is there any way to finish the story tonight?"

Lois turned her attention from Sara to her new friend's father.

"John", her confidence quieted the room, "I believe you are exactly where you need to be right now."

She looked him in the eye and squared her shoulders. "I know it's important to you to get going and it maybe that you are supposed to get on the road in the morning, but have you considered that this is where the Lord wants you all right now?"

John looked at her with a touch of confusion, "Well, no, I..."   Lois interrupted before he could continue, "Would you be willing, right now as a family, based on all that's happened, to pray and ask the Lord?" John looked at the rest of his family seated around the table. Each gave a small nod of ascent. He was concerned about getting through this trip and back home, but could see his family did not share his concern.

"Alright, alright. We will pray and do whatever we're told." He motioned for his clan to follow him. They stopped in the foyer near the front of the house making a small circle and holding hands as they prayed. "Father" he began, but got no further as he felt a peace and assurance fall on him like a mantle, heavy but comforting. Without realizing it, he reverently closed with "Amen." He opened his eyes to see his wife and children looking at him as if he'd had a small stroke.

"What?" He shrugged self-consciously, "The Lord answered my prayer before it began." Annie's lifted eyebrow told him she wanted more information but he simply tugged on her hand and motioned for the kids to follow as he walked back into the dining room.

"We'll stay one more day", he announced loudly. "Can you recommend a hotel nearby?"

Lois smiled and she was transformed. Her former beauty, which had been erased with age and life, shone through. "Why, you're going to stay with me of course!" After some arguing, polite refusals and intercession from Pastor Wallen, John put his trust in the Lord and agreed that the family would stay the night with Lois.

Wedner Farm Nebraska, 2001 12:30 am

Sara opened her eyes to blackness. Fear and confusion tilted her vision.

"Where am I?"

She looked around a darkened room. As her eyes adjusted to the blackness she realized she was in Lois' guestroom. What had woken her? Then she heard it, voices rising from downstairs. Why were her parents still awake?

She got out of bed quietly trying not to cause any creaks in the wooden floor. Putting on her slippers, she walked to the door, opened it slowly and looked out into the hall. Darkness. Her eyes shifted to the end of the hall where the stairs led to the first floor. There was a faint light coming through the stairwell, and Sara tiptoed quietly towards it, straining her ears.

She knew it was wrong to eavesdrop, and she repeated this to herself as she crept stealthily toward the stairs. Any kid will tell you though, she reminded herself, as she snuck quietly down the stairs, sometimes it's the only way to learn anything, especially when you're the youngest. As she got closer to the bottom she strained to hear what was being discussed.

"We kill them tonight."

Sara froze like a statue as the words were repeated softly, over and over, with such evil intent that she stuffed her pajama top in her mouth to keep from screaming. Slowly, like a bucket at the bottom of the well being raised, she stood to her feet. Panic. Don't Panic. Panic!

She turned to rush back upstairs when a creak in the floor boards screeched an alarm at her feet. She instantly froze again, listening.

There was quiet for a moment and then the litany started again, only this time it was moving!

She heard the dining room door to the kitchen swing open on its hinges. This was followed by deep scratching sounds as if a large bear were walking toward the hallway from the dining room.

Her feet finally caught up with her fear and she flew up the stairs towards her parents' room. Panic and fear scrambled her reason and she raced to the left, entering the room at the end of the hall, opening and shutting the door behind her and breathing heavily.

"Wha…What…whose there?" Lois' voice came softly out of the dark, confused and small.

It made Sara jump and give a little "chirp" of fear.

"Sara, is that you honey?" When Sara didn't immediately respond, Lois patted the bed next to her, "Come on honey come over here." Sara raced to the side of the bed, kicking a table with her little toe and falling on her butt right where Lois had patted the bed.

"Lois, Lois, hurry we need to get to my parents room! Someone…thing's in the house. It has claws and its saying kill them all tonight!" Lois sat up in bed, but Sara was not sensing any alarm. She slowly took Sara into her arms.

"Let's pray."

Sara tried to pull away. Lois obviously was still half asleep and not comprehending the severity of the situation. As with all the many surprises of Lois, she became strong as an ox and held onto Sara to keep her from bolting.

"Shh, shh, listen Sara, listen."

Sara finally stopped struggling to get away and listened. A great crunching noise came from the stairs. Something large was breaking the stairs as it came for them! Sara froze and Lois turned to her in the dark so that her mouth was against Sara's ear.

"That is Fear, Sara. Bow your head, quickly."

Sara responded to her friend's command, leaning her head into Lois' small frail body.

"Dear Lord, God of all, we rebuke this demon in the name of Jesus Christ, we grab hold of your love and relinquish our fear in Your Good Name, amen." Instantaneously, the crunching on the stairs ceased. Sara sat up startled, as much by the silence, as she had been by the noises that had driven her to Lois' room.

"Uh, uh, is…is it gone?" Sara breathed against Lois' crispy short hair.

Lois laughed quietly and patted Sara's hand. "Yes, it is gone. You just relax. Everything is fine and we are more than safe." Sara blinked and rubbed her eyes when Lois reached over and turned on her bedside light. As the spots dissolved, Sara looked at Lois. Her friend looked so old, so small in the shadowy light.

"Lois please, please I need to know what that thing was."

Lois shifted on her queen-size mattress and invited Sara to recline next to her. "Baby girl, I've been dealing with Fear for most of my life. It likes to tramp through my house and make a lot of noise, but I don't give place to it here anymore."

Sara looked in Lois' eyes and saw a giggle lurking.

"I still don't understand, is that thing real? It sounded so real."

The look in Lois' eyes turned from laughter to something hard, something Sara had not seen there before.

"They are very real Sara, don't ever doubt it! Doubt and Fear are two of the most paralyzing weapons Satan uses against us." She shifted in her bed slightly, giving Sara more room, before continuing.   "Satan is a supreme being, a principality if you will, who feels he lost his inheritance to what he considers lower life forms. He has watched and learned and rules with an iron fist all those under his control, like Fear, Chaos, The Random..." here Lois closed her eyes and said a quick 'Jesus'.

"I believe that you are being pursued by this last demon...Random...if I'm right, you Sara, are a very important piece to our Lord's plan."

Sara jumped out of the bed and paced back and forth waving her hands and speaking rapidly, "I am not important, I am fifteen, I'm a kid." Her agitation was like a whirlwind in a washing machine and the older wiser woman almost laughed.

Instead Lois grabbed her hand as she passed by and Sara stopped to look at her with an eyebrow raised and tears rebelling at the corners of her lovely brown eyes, looking much like the proverbial deer caught in the headlights.

"Our purpose comes to us whether we like it or not."

This profound statement hit Sara squarely in her frontal cortex. Her tears finally slipped free of their shelter and began to fall unchecked down her cheeks. Sara slipped quietly back on the bed and leaned into Lois' shoulder.

"I'm not prepared for anything like this AT ALL!" A wail punctuated her feelings.

Lois pulled her close and kissed the top of her head. "I know that is what you believe, but tomorrow when I finish my story, I hope you will change your mind just a little. Remember, I was all alone when the Lord called me, terrified just doesn't sound like a strong enough word does it?" Sara shook her head back and forth, calmed a bit by Lois' words.

"I don't think I'll be able to get back to sleep though."

Lois pulled the covers up over both of them, reaching over to turn out the light. "You just close your eyes and rest. I'll keep my ears open for anymore disturbances." Doing as she was told, Sara kissed Lois' silken paper-thin cheek, and closed her eyes.

When she opened them again, she was alone in Lois' bed. The sun was shining through two lovely vista windows overlooking the barn and horse corral directly into Sara's eyes. She sat up quickly, able to see the layout of her friend's room. A layout that had been shadowed last night when she'd run in. There was such peace and happiness in this room; a feeling, more than the look of things.

"O.k. Jesus, I'm not as scared in the light. Help me please to not be afraid." She jumped from the bed and opening the door walked into the hall.

Her stomach grumbled a little as she looked at the open door to the room where her parents had slept. Stepping lightly, she walked to the doorway, and looked in the room. Her mother was bent over the bed tucking the corner of a quilted coverlet against the wall.

"Morning mom." Sara smiled. "How'd you guys sleep?"

Annie jumped just a little at her daughter's voice before turning her head to look at her.

Sara was relieved to see her mom was smiling. "Your father and I slept like rocks! I thought Lois must've slipped us a mickey."

"What's a mickey?" Sara asked with a look of utter confusion on her face.

Annie laughed again, "It's just an expression for drugging someone's drink."

Sara paused, "Really! Do you think Lois might do something like that? I don't think she would mom, I went to her room last night when Fear was tramping up the stairs and I..."

"What?!" Annie nearly yelled, Sara now having her full attention.

"It's o.k. mom, Lois is going to explain everything at breakfast this morning. I'm pretty sure though she didn't spit on your mickey." and with that she turned and walked down the stairs where the smells of bacon and maple syrup wafted from below.

Annabelle stood in the center of the room and realized a moment of panic as she had an overwhelming sensation of stepping into someone else's life. What the haymaker was going on?!

"Lord, Lord!" her spirit cried out. "I am afraid and way outside of my element of normalcy. I need you to help me accept this! Please be a light to my feet in this darkness. Amen."

Annie turned back and finished making the bed before heading down to what promised to be the most interesting breakfast of her life.

Outside of time

These circles are closing.

The Morning Star worked intrinsically in circles; crop circles, government circles, circles that curved into themselves and repeated patterns allowing for some sense of omniscience.

The old woman was crafty but old.

One thing I, The Random have learned, is the circle is closing, as circles do, and outside of time precision is needed to assure the circle closes as the Fallen One desires. Nebraska is lovely this time of year.

Chapter 11

2001 Wedner Farm, Nebraska 10:00 am

The Beloved family sat back from the table each rubbing over-full tummies or burping behind their hands and blushing.

It had been a truly bountiful breakfast. John and Annie, who were ready to get on the road, felt Lois had planned it that way so that she could finish her incredulous story without interruption.

"Ms. Wedner, John began, but her hand coming up in a halting motion made him stop and begin again.

"Lois, I know we are waiting on the Pastor, but we really…"

Lois stood. "Mr. Beloved…John", she smiled at her joke, "the pastor will be here in about five minutes. He can smell my cookin' from the church." another chuckle.

I am more than willing to begin now. I'll have plenty of time to fill in the pastor… (before *we* leave, she thought to herself)…lets go into the parlor and get comfortable before I continue…anymore coffee anyone?"

Annie raised her hand like a child as she stood from the table.

"Can I help with that Lois?"

Lois smiled a yes and Annie followed her into the kitchen. She stood back and watched Lois move around her kitchen in a dance and envied her. Annie had never been one for the kitchen. She cooked the basics and really wished she had a love for it like her mother or Lois, but she did everything backwards and worked sixty hours a week which usually meant eating out or

Stouffer's lasagna for dinner. Lois however, looked as if she were born to be there.

The kitchen was lit by the sun shining through the window, and Annie after having seen what she had in these last few days, was not surprised to see (imagine?) that a halo of light surrounded Lois' head as she worked.

Lois turned to Annie with a cup of coffee in an earthen brown mug in her hand.

"Here ya go honey, I think we left the cream and sugar in the dining room."

Annie set the coffee cup on the butcher block in the center of the kitchen and lightly laid her hand on Lois' shoulder as the older woman walked past her toward the swinging doors to the dining room. Lois turned toward her with a smile on her face and a question in her eyes, "Yes dear?"

Annie started to speak, but then closed her mouth again. She wanted to ask her what was going on, and why her daughter was talking about fear tramping upstairs, but instead, her spirit was stirred and she hugged her and whispered "thank you" in her ear before she grabbed her coffee from the block and turned with her to leave the kitchen.

The rest of the Beloved's waited in the parlor. It was a beautifully appointed room at the back of the house with a large fireplace taking up much of the space of one wall and a large picture window that looked out on the rolling hills behind the farm. Each looked up expectantly as the two women entered.

"Ok", Lois began, "who is ready to finish this story?" Four hands shot up like stones headed for Goliath.

Between Sante Fe and Roswell New Mexico, 1950

Lois rode in Papa Gus' new Chevy truck headed south to Roswell, to a revival.

The road they travelled had been paved only last year. Lois was miserable from the heat of the day, but at least there was no flying dust or jutting bumps to contend with.

She was lucky however. She was sandwiched between Papa Gus and Mama Angel in the front seat and so her mouth was not full of fumes and bugs like her adopted siblings who sat in the back under a stretched tarp. She wished she felt lucky.

She had told Mama Angel that she was going to make the journey alone. She knew how to drive and would have no problem making the three and one half hour trip on her own (more like five since Raymond and Ernesto had to stop every two minutes to go to the bathroom).

Mama Angel just smiled. "I don't think so Niña. That is a lot of desert to be getting lost in and I wouldn't be able to sleep. Besides, I want to go to the revival." and with that she had ended the subject.

So here she sat sticking with perspiration glue to each of her loving yet large adopted parents on her way to meet…her what?

The Lord spoke softly in her spirit, "Your purpose."

Two hours into the ride and they were approaching the mountains just outside of Roswell.

Clouds had been gathering all day and it began to sprinkle. This made Papa Gus very happy. He'd been waiting for an excuse to use his new

Folberths; an automatic device that allowed him to clear the rain from the windshield.

Lois stared straight ahead. She was tired and wanted a bathroom break, but after chiding the two young boys for "making us late", she knew she'd hold it til they got there, or die trying.

She floated from thought to thought like the breeze from Papa Gus' open window. Ahead a desert panorama stretched out in front of her; sand colors mixed with high desert oranges and blues. Lois' eyes began to close drowsily.

It seemed she had just begun to doze off when she was thrown violently against the dashboard of the truck striking her head. Lois heard three loud 'thuds' in the back of the truck and she turned to Gus her fear making her shout, "What are you doing!"

But Papa Gus just stared straight ahead, his chest resting on the steering wheel, his foot crunching the brake. As she stared at him blankly, all Lois could think was "he's had a stroke."

Papa Gus' mouth hung slack.   Frozen, it seemed to Lois' confused mind, as if it had come unhinged. Through the fifteen seconds it had taken for all of this to occur, Lois had not once turned to look at Mama. Now she felt fear coil itself in the pit of her stomach because she knew if Mama was o.k. she would have been the first to shout.

In shock and terrified she slowly turned her head to the right, praying like a child begging away the boogeyman, for Mama to be alright. Her head stopped in mid-turn when her eyes caught a glimpse of something through the windshield and her mouth opened in a silent scream.

Outside of time

The time of the 'new land beginning', as it is called in this circle, ironically begins in a desolate wasteland. A desert road on a deserted highway.

Ironic, because this will be the face of the new reign; stretches of desolation punctuated by moments of terror and death. They will stumble to their destruction. They will beg for our mercy and receive the virus we spread into their DNA like an offering.

Oh but the time is nigh, yes even at the door. The Vine is returned, the Graft is a child. Now are birth pangs squeezing out our victory. RANDOM!

Kept in a dark cell yearning for release, only allowed out each millennium. Now unleashed to fulfill my purpose…his purpose, until the time of times…

***

Highway 285 – 80 miles north of Roswell NM 1950

Lois could not explain what she was seeing.

The only thing human about it were a head, torso, arms and legs. It was extraordinarily tall and whitish-gray in color, and stared at the truck like it was an insect through eyes that took up two thirds of its face. There was no blinking; just a cold stare of hatred that permeated the truck and made Mama moan out loud…Mama!

Lois, with great effort and some fear, pulled her eyes from the being, and as if in a critical sequence from a movie, continued to turn her head in slow motion to look at Mama Angel. Lois gasped horrified at what she found. When the truck had stopped suddenly Mama's head was flung violently into the passenger window. A shard of glass approximately four inches wide at the top and narrowing to a one inch jagged knife at the bottom, stuck ghoulishly out of Mama's right eye.

Lois almost vomited on first seeing it, but a flash of glee, felt not heard, made her anger boil as she turned her head back to the windshield. The being was still staring at the vehicle, nothing had changed, except Lois sensed a delight, a glee at the tragedy playing out in the truck.

The elements of her world irrevocably shifted in that moment. The being was not emoting by facial changes or body language…it had none, yet Lois felt a buzzing at her ear, an itching, similar to other times in her life when she felt a little crazy… like after her grandparents death when people would speak to her and all she could hear was noise.

Very similar, except this time the evil intent behind the buzzing was extremely loud and close, like breath on her face, making her want to reach both hands up to her ears and scratch them until they bled.

The monster had not moved. Not a twitch. It stood in the middle of the road looking at them like ants, like bugs that should be squashed, but did not move. Lois took the opportunity to turn around and look through the glass into the back of the truck. The children lay in a heap like broken dolls. Arms and legs at odd angles and little Ernesto on the top of the pile staring at her but not saying anything…

"NO!"

Lois screamed it though she was not aware of it, or the muttered, "no…no…no…no" that became a litany in her head and on her lips. "LORD Jesus help me!"

The torment was wrenched from her gut in anguish and she was only aware of a flash and a shimmer before the being... that evil malicious being...disappeared. Lois felt herself snap out of the slow motion movie as the lightning and shimmering disappeared. She turned first to Papa Gus who still stared transfixed at the spot in the road where the being had just stood.

"Papa...Papa" Lois patted his cheeks at first as she called to him. He would not look at her or even acknowledge that she was there. Her pats became slaps as she tried harder to snap him out of his stupor,

"PAPA!" This time when she yelled it, he blinked rapidly and shook his head several times, muttering incomprehensible words in Spanglish. Finally he turned to her and said quietly (as only gentle Papa Gus could), "Are we there Niña...did I fall asleep?"

Lois was becoming frustrated because it felt as if hours had passed since Papa had slammed on his brakes. So she answered him a little too sharply, "Don't you remember?!"

He looked at her sleepily and she noticed for the first time a large lump beginning to form on the left side of his head near his temple. It reduced her anger to the fear that had caused it and she put her hands gently on his face and looked into his eyes before she spoke again.

"We've had an accident Papa." She was surprised by how calm and steady her voice sounded as she waited for his reply. When none was forthcoming, she pulled his face closer.

"We need to hurry, we need to get to a hospital", this said calmly too although with more urgency and emphasized by a low moan from Mama beside her, but still there was no response.

Lois knew she couldn't wait any longer. She let go of Papa's face and let his head loll back on the headrest.

Moving slowly and carefully she crawled over Papa's lap and opening the door, jumped out of the truck. She rushed around to the other side where Mama's head rested against the broken window.   She knew she needed to find something to wrap around Mama's head to keep it still. The road was paved but could be bumpy in spots where flash flooding had pitted and scarred the asphalt. The answer came to her like a blessing.

She removed the small sweater she wore and reached through the broken glass to wrap Mama's head.   She pulled it tight; relying on the small amount of first aid training Mama had taught her.   Once she had secured the jacket around Mama's head like a turban, she ran back to the other side of the truck.

Papa's eyes were closed and his mouth remained slack. Lois grabbed hold of the frame of the truck door and in a sitting position pushed Papa into the middle seat with her body weight.

He fell to his right coming to rest on Mama's shoulder. Lois turned the engine of the truck over and looked at the road ahead.   A brief shimmering began to wave the air where the creature had stood and it was all the invitation that Lois needed as she put the truck into first gear and punched the gas pedal.

Chapter 12

The drive to Roswell seemed to Lois like a trip through hell. Endless time spent in fear and panic. Overcome with grief and hot air burning her lungs, choking her.

She wouldn't think about the children in the back. The quiet was deafening and she was sure they were already dead. She shook the thought away from her head physically to keep from throwing up and did all that was left to her...she prayed.

"Lord, what is this? Did you save my life to give me more pain? Did you bring me to love these people only so I could watch them all die!!??" Silence. No little voice like she'd come to expect, no warming in her heart to reassure. She was alone in the desert of her fears.

"I NEED HELP!"

She was crying hysterically barely able to see the road in front of her. As she drove almost one hundred miles an hour toward Roswell, she missed the sign letting her know she was only ten miles away now. She also missed the highway patrolman sitting on the side of the road in his car eating a hero sandwich for lunch.

**

Carl Wedner had just put his Gracie Mae (a local diner in town) sandwich to his lips. He'd waited all day before going to buy the sandwich. He only allowed himself one a week. His Sergeant James Tagman had an intimate relationship with Gracie Mae's sandwiches and his gut stretched so wide across his belted pants it looked like a teardrop ready to fall.

Just as he was about to sink his teeth into the first bite (the best bite!), a late model GMC truck went whooshing by at well over the posted speed limit, causing him to quickly move the sandwich away from his mouth and drop its guts all over his lap! He dropped the rest of the sandwich in disgust and swore, smacking his hands on the steering wheel as he did.

"Oh ho ho, you are mine mister." It came out as a curse. Starting up his cruiser, he called in his location and pursuit to the main office in Roswell. He took off skidding out of the dirt on the side of the road and punching the pedal to try and catch the truck. He had a moment of panic when he saw a small head bob up out of the back of the truck for just a moment before it disappeared from sight.

This enraged Carl to the point of wanting to literally kill the person driving the truck once he had it pulled over...and he would pull it over! His lights and sirens blaring, he roared up next to the truck only to be struck dumb by the Angel sitting in the driver's seat.

"No, not an angel", he thought, a demon disguised as an angel...what angel would drive at this speed with children in the back of a truck?" When the angel continued to ignore him, he grabbed his car radio, switched on his loudspeaker and ordered her to "Pull Over!"

He thought she would ignore him at first as she had not even acknowledged he was there but kept her eyes forward unblinking.

Suddenly however she glanced to her left and saw his car riding alongside hers and for the first time he could see her eyes as blue as a cloudless sky, but empty...shock, she was in shock! He'd seen that look before during the war. Carl honked his horn steadily hoping to make her focus on him and she finally did looking him directly in the eye through their windows.

He mouthed the words "Pull Over" and noticed the truck begin to slow as she downshifted and finally stopped. She didn't wait for him to come to the truck window however, but jumped out instead and ran toward him.

Carl felt momentary shame because his first thought as she flew toward him was "Beautiful."

He shook himself mentally and opened the car door ready to admonish (no longer bent on strangling) when Lois stopped him short.

"Please... please help me... help me sir...my family they're dead or dying, they need help...help me please!" Carl grabbed her to him. "To calm her", he told himself. It was wrong, it was not regulation, but she needed him, he felt it.

"O.k. ma'am o.k.", his voice was a calm whisper as he held her to his chest protectively, "its o.k., tell me what's wrong, its o.k." and he felt her melt into him and slump into his shirt.

She began to speak broken words against his chest...

"Man, not man, something evil...in the road...slammed on brakes, everyone hurt or dead, I don't know....need help please" and she began to sob. Carl was able to deduce from her broken words that there had been an accident and that the child he had seen and maybe others were hurt and needed help.

"Listen to me ma'am. Ma'am?"

The young woman looked into his eyes and he could see forlornness in them so heavy, it broke his heart into a million pieces and made him want to shelter and protect her.

"What's your name?" he whispered tenderly.

"Lois, why?" she rebuked, making Carl bark a little laugh at her toughness.

"Lois, I'm going to go check on everyone in the truck. I need you to sit right here in the car until I get back. Can you do that for me?" She nodded as if her head weighed twenty pounds and he could see she was descending into her safe place as her eyes shuttered blank.

He took her by the shoulders and shook her. "Lois, Lois, listen to me!"

She swatted at his face to make the noise go away so she could sleep, mmm sleep. "What was she doing awake again? And who was the person who kept yelling her name like he knew her?"

She felt herself fall back on the seat of the highway patrolman's driver's side, and popped up like a prairie dog.

She heard rather than felt a 'whoosh' of air come through her lungs and she opened her eyes.

"Where was she?" Lois briefly looked around and took in the patrol car, her legs hanging out the front driver's door, blood on her dress...Mama! Papa!

She stood and half ran half limped back to the truck where she could see an officer climbing into the back of Papa Gus' truck. "When had he shown up? Was it another of the alien beings? Was he trying to take the children!?"

"Hey, hey get out of that truck!" Her scream was hysterical and she was sure the creature had come back to hurt them. The officer turned and jumped down at her voice. Lois was sure she was losing her mind when he looked at her because all she could think was "beautiful".

"Lois", she heard spoken from his lips, "it's alright, I'm Patrolman Wedner."

He walked toward her slowly and she did not realize until he reached for her arm that she had been walking backward away from him as he moved. His touch was gentle and calmed her and she stopped frozen in the dirt on the side of the road. "I'm here to help you Lois. I need you to get back in the truck and follow me. I'm going to get us to the hospital, o.k.? Can you do that?"

The first words past her lips were "Beautiful."

Carl took this as an affirmative and led her back to the truck, helping her inside and closing the door. "Lois", he said calmly, reassuringly. She turned at the sound of his voice and looked into his eyes. He almost forgot what they were talking about but was shaken by the urgency surrounding them. "Follow me, do you understand?" She nodded and turned the truck over.

Carl jogged back to his cruiser. He could not get the site of the children in the back of the truck out of his mind. They literally littered the bed of the truck and not one of them was conscious.

He jumped into the patrol car, slammed it into gear and began driving toward Roswell with his car radio in his hand. He glanced up to see if Lois was following. The truck stuttered and jerked before she was able to get it into the right gear, but soon she was following close.

"Good girl", he thought and then depressed the button on the radio to explain to the patrol office his extraordinary experience and where he was headed.

"Maria, I want you to see if we can get our other patrol cars to line the street downtown so we don't hit any traffic, I've got several injuries, most serious, maybe fatal.

He could almost see Maria shaking her head back and forth.

"O.k. Carl, but I don't think Sergeant Tagman's gonna like you putting his cars somewhere without asking." He knew she was probably right, but Carl couldn't explain how important it was right now. In fact he wasn't sure why he thought it was so important, but there was a stirring in his soul that had been missing for some time. A stirring he knew came from God. Carl Wedner felt something so foreign he almost physically pushed it away…compassion.

He had buried his compassion at Normandy and had no interest in digging it up, but he felt tears burn the back of his eyes as he flashed on the children in the back of the truck he'd just climbed into. "I'll take the blame, just please call St. Mary's and have them ready. I have two adults …three total…but two needing assistance with serious but what looks like non-life threatening injuries and three maybe four children with"…Maria interrupted him, "What do you mean three maybe four Carl! Is it three or four?"

"That's what I've been trying to tell you!" He took a deep breath, apologizing before continuing "The children are in a pile in the back of the truck Maria", and he sobbed, "Please, just make sure they're ready. Maria, who heard the depth of heartbreak in Carl's voice, did not say another word other than 'out' and got busy making the calls.

***

Twenty minutes later both the truck and the patrol car pulled up to the front of the hospital.

Several nurses, a doctor and three nuns stood at the bay doors ready to help. Lois jumped from the truck and ran to the passenger door. Attendants appeared out of nowhere (as far as Lois could tell) and began to load her adopted parents and siblings onto gurneys and wheel them into the hospital.

Carl stood at the back of the truck and watched as they pulled Ernesto out first. His eyes were lifeless. He was gone. The other three children who had come on the trip were put on stretchers as well and wheeled away.

Lois could not have said when Patrolman Wedner came and put his arm around her to lead her into the hospital, or how she got into a hospital bed. So she was completely thrown off guard when she opened her eyes again to find him sitting at the foot of her bed with his head bent forward and his eyes shut as if he was praying.

"Hello" came from her mouth in a breathy whisper, but loud enough for him to lift his head and smile at her.

"Lois, hello!" he grinned at her and through her misery she grinned back feeling she had no choice. "Why does he keep using my given name like he knows me?" Her irritation made her next question sound accusatory. "Please tell me about my family, I can take it, it's why you're here isn't it? To tell me they're all de...dea...dead" her sobs wracked her as she grabbed her head in her hands. He was next to her in an instant; taking liberties by gently taking one of her hands from her head and squeezing it.

"No! No!" he reassured, "no one is dead!"

Lois' head shot up. "You're lying! I saw Ernesto! He was gone!"

How was he going to explain this? In all of his years in the army and his few as a patrolman in his home town, Carl had seen a lot of death. In his life as a Christian, he had never...NEVER...imagined he would actually witness a miracle.

He went to church every Sunday where he always left an offering. He thanked the "Man Upstairs" for all his blessings and prayed when those he loved were in trouble, but he'd never seen a miracle... until today.

After the attendants had wheeled in Lois' family (although they were obviously Hispanic and she was not), the children had been taken into separate curtained areas. The adult male was taken into a curtained area, but the adult female was immediately moved to their surgical area.

As Carl stood in the hallway watching the frenzied activity, he began to hear children crying in fear or pain, he couldn't tell if it was either or both, but it gave him hope. Bright like a shining star in his chest. Noise is good. Crying is good, it meant life. Slowly he made his way to each curtained space and looked in.

A little girl about thirteen years old was holding her arm as she rocked back and forth repeating "Mama, mama." A little boy around ten or eleven with a large scrape up the back of his calf and thigh let tears run down his face as he licked a lollipop one of the nurses brought in.

The next to the last curtained area is where Carl found Ernesto. His small brown body was limp and lifeless. The doctors and nurses had been trying for several minutes to revive him; he did not respond.

As Carl pulled back the curtain, he watched as the nuns standing on either side of the small boy began to pray. Carl was not catholic and did not recognize their prayers, but recognized they were calling on the God of the universe for help. He responded inwardly, like a tug that pulled him over to the bed of the child.

The burning sensation clogged the back of his eyes again as he stared at the little boy pale and lifeless and small on the bed…and Carl felt the tug again. He bent over the bed…he was not aware of it. The nuns began to protest, but an elderly nun who seemed to have some authority, waved them back and encouraged them to keep praying.

Carl kissed Ernesto's forehead and laid his hand on his chest, and then he did the oddest thing…he could only explain later that a still small voice, a voice he couldn't deny or stop spoke in his soul… "Breath of life", and hearing these words, he stooped over and breathed into little Ernesto's mouth, feeling the child's cold lips pressed to his. As the breath left his mouth, Carl felt warmth and heat and sizzling. Like an electrical line, like lightning. All the hairs on his body stood on end and he felt a buzzing in the room.

Carl fell backward onto the floor as the small precious child sucked in air! Little Ernesto sucked in oxygen like a newborn making its introduction into the world.

Every adult in the room audibly sucked in their breath like a vacuum, as if the boy's breath had stolen theirs.

The nuns, in an orderly fashion, dropped to their knees, furiously saying their rosary and thanking God. Carl, being a little more practical in the moment screamed for "a doctor, a doctor please!"

Now as he sat next to Lois, he was unable, maybe a little embarrassed, to admit what had happened to Ernesto, and the role he had played in it. "Lois", he began, but was interrupted when she chimed in.

"I don't believe we've been properly introduced, I am Lois Cantor... you may call me Miss Cantor."

Carl listened to Lois in her prim and proper voice dress him down for being so familiar, and he was sure that when his heart thudded a little harder that it was love falling into his chest.

"I do apologize" he smiled at her, "Miss Cantor." She gave a little nod and began again.

He explained what had happened in the little emergency room. He felt relaxed when he spoke, and was not afraid, not with her.

The miraculous nature of his explanation brought sudden tears to his eyes...he who hadn't shed a tear for the fallen in Normandy, as he a Corpsman, stormed through the blood and bullets with his unit, feeling useless to help as one fell fatally after another, until he and his lieutenant were all that remained at the top of the hill.

Lois, taken aback at this show of emotion for her little brother, grabbed his hand to comfort him...and felt lightning and shimmering! Surprised, she immediately let go, and rubbed her hand where it still tingled. Carl...Patrolman Wedner... felt it too. She could tell by the pleasure in his eyes (or was that a deeper emotion), and the way he too rubbed his hand.

"Miss Cantor", he began hesitantly, "I am not sure what happened with Ernesto, or what happened between us just now, but I won't try to deny either. I believe to deny it might make the 'Man Upstairs' look away from this moment and I won't have that either."

Lois, who'd become uncharacteristically silent, felt unsure and inexplicably thrilled. She didn't know this man from Adam, yet when he looked at her that way, and spoke of miracles and something between she and him, she became a little flushed, a little girlish, as if she should blush, slap him lightly on the hand while simpering, and telling him to "stop that." Instead, she looked him in the eye and asked "where are Mama Angel and Papa Gus?"

Carl knew the question was coming. He did not want to tell her that her Papa Gus had a stroke and was being cared for but was unresponsive. He didn't want to mention that her Mama Angel had lost her right eye, and remained delirious repeating "demon be gone, demon be gone."

He didn't want to, but when she looked at him, he could not hide it, would not hide it from her. So he took a deep breath and gave an accounting of her family.

Lois didn't wail or scream or call him a liar again. She simply turned her back to him and cried to the wall. Carl reached out to give her comfort. His hand went to her shoulder before he was even aware of it, but he pulled up short

and shook his head. He would let her grieve.
She needed rest.

He would just have to come back, he decided.
She still had questions to answer. For instance,
why in the middle of the desert, with no other
cars in sight, had her Papa Gus slammed on his
brakes?

***

A few hours after Patrolman Wedner left the
room, Lois lost her mind. She began to call out
loudly "Papa Gus! Mama Angel!" A nun/nurse
came into the room to quiet her down. She had
a syringe in her right hand. Lois sat up in the
hospital bed with her arms outstretched in
supplication,

"No, no I don't need that!" Lois' eyes rolled a
little wildly but she continued her plea, "I need
to see Mama Angel! Please, please I can walk,
please just take me to her!"   Sister Anna-
Therese, the older nun Carl had seen earlier that
appeared to be in charge, looked at the beautiful
young girl on the bed and her heart melted just a
little. She stuck the syringe in the pocket of the
lab coat she wore over her Habit.

"Alright" the sister said looking at Lois
carefully, "your Mama should be ready to
receive a visitor. Get dressed and I'll take you
to her room." Lois popped from the bed like
popcorn on a fire and pulled on the dress she'd
been wearing when the accident occurred. It
was caked in blood in spots from trying to help
her family, but she didn't notice. Sister Anna-
Therese did.

"We'll get you something to wear first o.k.?"
She smiled at Lois who looked down at her
dress and frowned. "That would be wonderful,
thank you sister...?"

"Anna-Therese, but you may call me Sister Anna."

"Thank you Sister Anna."

With the introductions over and Lois dressed in a novice habit left by a young woman who loved the Lord, but loved the thought of marriage to Julio a little more, they walked toward the room where Mama Angela lay sleeping.

"I'll leave you here", Sister Anna said quietly. Lois turned around and hugged her and thanked her before walking slowly into the room. She didn't recognize her precious Mama at first. There were two beds and the first had a woman wrapped from head to toe in bandages whose left arm was missing. "Did they take Mama's arm?!"

Lois' heart raced at the thought, but then she noticed blond hair peeking out from the bandages on her head. "Whew! That's not Mama." She breathed a sigh of relief as her feet took her closer to the bed near the window.

This woman's head was wrapped, but the rest of her body was not and she could see by the careworn hands that it was indeed her Mama! She grabbed a metal chair that sat in a corner and scraped it along the floor as she pulled it up alongside her Mama's bed. The noise from the chair brought movement from the bed as Angela's head began to swing back and forth. She muttered "Demon be gone, demon be gone", and began to cried softly "my babies, my babies."

Lois leaned over the rails of her bed and began to stroke the side of her face through the bandages swaddled around her head.

"Mama, mama, it's me, it's your Niña Lois."

Mama Angel's head swung slowly toward Lois' voice and she wailed softly, "Niña, Niña, gone, gone everyone is gone, all is lost..." Lois realized Angela was still sedated. She didn't know that everyone was alright. Leaning close to her ear, Lois whispered, "No Mama, everyone is o.k., no one is gone." This seemed to calm Mama Angel a little, and so she began to repeat the words over her like a prayer, stroking her arm and shoulder and bandaged face in turn.   When Mama sat up abruptly, as if pushed to a sitting position by some unseen force, Lois leapt out of her chair.

Lois called out for help, crying for the nurses, but the sound came out as lifeless air. Angela looked possessed. Her head turned slowly towards Lois, and she directed her stare at her adopted daughter with her good eye. Lois stared to approach her, when Mama raised her right arm, pointed her finger at Lois and declared, "You must go to the revival!" "You must go tonight!" before falling back to the bed in a heap.

"Mama, mama!" Lois cried, "Help! Help, my mother needs help!" This time her words came out as a scream and the doctor rushed in followed by Sister Anna.   Lois was shoved rudely out of the way as the doctor bent over Angela. He examined her bandages, her one good eye and listened to her heartbeat before turning to Lois.

"What is the matter with you?!" The doctor was stern and cross looking.   "You do not scream for help unless someone is dying do you understand me young lady!?"

"But...but..." Lois stuttered, "She sat up! She talked to me, and then she fell back on the bed!"

"Impossible!   She is heavily sedated, and doubtless has no idea you're even here! Sister Anna, please take this young lady back to her room and keep her there!" The doctor stomped out of the room muttering about 'days like today' as Sister Anna walked over to Lois who was upset and just a little angry and put her arm around her steering her toward the door.

"What did your Mama say to you dear that got you so upset?"

Lois sniffled, "She said I have to go to the revival tonight.   That's why we were driving here."

Sister Anna nodded her head, she was aware of the revival. It was always a topic of conversation at dinner in the abbey when Protestants were holding a revival.

"I can't go now though!   I can't leave them all here to go to a church revival!"

Sister Anna smiled knowingly, "My dear that is the perfect time to go to a church revival. Let's see if we can't find you some clothes to wear."

Chapter 13

A dress that fit reasonably well and sandals were found in the donation bin in the back of the hospital near the Abbey. Lois returned to the room they had given her to change her clothes, only to find Carl Wedner...Patrolman Wedner sitting on the edge of the bed looking forlorn.

He popped like a weasel and grabbed his patrolman's hat off his head. "I really am sorry Miss Cantor. I was just sitting here wondering if you'd left to return to your real family when you came in and look here you are heh, heh." His head dipped in embarrassment at being caught sitting on her bed.

"Patrolman Wedner..." her voice was softer now he noticed. "I appreciate your concern, I do, but..."

Carl raised his hand and brought a finger to his lips.

Was he shushing her!? Lois began to open her mouth to upbraid his gumption, but he just shook his head back and forth holding his finger up. She almost laughed, but quietly raised an eyebrow at him waiting for him to continue.

"First, and humbly, I would like to ask that you call me Carl."

Lois began to open her mouth to tell him what she thought of his request, but his finger was back at his mouth and he was shaking his head again.

"Next, I spoke with Sister Anna before coming by your room, and would like to request that you allow me to escort you to the church revival this evening, as I myself feel the need to be there. And last Miss Wedner; please allow me to use your given name."

Lois was struggling to keep a hold on her temper. What was it about this man that was making her jump from calm and collected to hopping mad in a matter of moments? It wasn't like her really. She took a deep breath, "Patro...Carl", he nodded encouragement to her.

"First let me tell you that Mama Angel and Papa Gus are my only family. My blood relations are all gone. Next, since I don't know where the tent revival is, I would be obliged for your help in getting there. Last, you may call me Lois, but don't go getting any ideas!"

Carl laughed, a rich rumbly sound that made Lois' knees bend in, just for a moment. When he spoke it was to tell her, "They could leave now if she was ready."

She looked down at her dress covered in blood and back at him, and they both laughed in unison. "I see, I see." He said turning a pretty shade of red at the thought of her changing her clothes. "I'll wait out in the hall until you're ready." And with that Carl walked quietly from the room.

Lois stood frozen for a moment. She was in a play. She was asleep. Her world seemed tilted. It seemed to her as though she were living in an alternate reality that did not belong to her. Would the Lord, who took her parents, and her grandparents, leave her alone again? These thoughts swirled in her head as she pulled on the dress she'd been given. Her grandmother's words "Don't dawdle" rang in her head as she hurried to finish dressing.

A small breeze lifted her hair and she turned quickly to see what had caused it. Nothing there.

Suddenly the bulb that swung from an industrial green lampshade caught her attention when it burned so brightly she had to shield her eyes with her hand and look away.

"Yep", she thought, "I've lost my mind." At that moment, at that very instant, she heard it. It was the same still small voice that had come to her in the hospital when she'd lost her grandparents. "He purposes to the cause of all who love Him."

This time however she answered back. "What purpose Lord, what purpose?!" Her tears came heavy as her legs folded under her and she came to rest on her knees.

The voice spoke again. "He claims you daughter of man; faith and patience, wisdom and understanding."

As before, Lois was calmed though nothing in her world seemed to have changed. Carl tapped on the door and opened it without being asked. Lois looked at him from her place on the floor with an angry question in her eyes.

"I heard you yelling, I didn't want to come in, but I did want to make sure you are safe."

Lois breathed out a large sigh before standing to put the sandals on her feet. "If you only knew Carl, you'd run as fast as you could away from here... away from me." Now it was Carl's turn to look an angry question at her.

"Excuse me Lois, but if you knew me, you'd know that I don't run."

She was taken aback at his response. Up until this time, Carl had been the epitome of kindness and politeness. A good patrolman who was concerned about the people he helped, but this response made her aware of him. Aware that he had made an extra effort to see that she and her family were cared for, that he had been there to tell her Ernesto was o.k., there to see how she was doing, there to make sure she got to the revival…

Did…did he like her?

A vague memory came to her in the instance before her response; of running toward him, of thinking 'beautiful'. She studied him now as the memory scurried through her head. Muscular and tall…at least six feet, brownish red hair that curled in different directions, even with the Brill Cream he'd put on it. Lois knew however she was most attracted to his green mossy eyes and wicked smile. They wrapped up who he was, kind and gentle, but dangerous.

"You're right Carl", she began, "I don't know you and I am very sorry if I offended you, it wasn't what I intended."

She stood from the floor on her own and held out her hand to shake his. "Hello, I'm Lois Cantor of Santa Fe, New Mexico." Her smile was bright and lit her whole countenance. Carl was instantly charmed back from the edge of effrontery.

He smiled back with genuine pleasure. "I'm Carl Wedner", he replied softly, "formerly of Albuquerque, New Mexico, now a resident of Roswell." Lois' eyes lit up at his statement, but she deferred the questions that rushed to her mouth and instead asked him "How long is the ride to the revival?"

He laughed his rumbly laugh, "about twenty minutes."

Lois looked down and realized they were still holding each other's hand and she pulled hers back clumsily. "Well, we'd better get going then."

The trip over in Carl's patrol car started quiet. Soon after however, Lois and Carl were talking like long lost friends who had "so much" to catch up on. With Carl's encouragement, Lois explained what had brought them to Roswell (only the tent revival, nothing of what had caused their accident), about Mama Angel and Papa Gus, her grandparents and finally her parents.

As her story moved along, Lois cried softly through the telling and Carl grabbed her hand across the leather bench seat in his cruiser and squeezed it to encourage her to continue.

When she was done, she wiped her eyes and smiled at him to show him she was o.k. Carl looked at her red eyes, runny nose and tear-stained face and his heart thumped over again. "She is beautiful."   To break the awkward silence Lois gave a little laugh and asked Carl, "So how about you Carl, what brought you to Roswell from lovely Albuquerque?"

To her dismay, the air in the car changed as a curtain of moodiness dropped over their window of discovery. "Well", he began quietly, slowly, as if he was about to speak about a subject he found repugnant, but quickly breathed a sigh of relief, "Oh look we're here."

Lois turned a troubled gaze to look out the front windshield. The car had stopped at an open field, and if she didn't know better, she would have believed he'd brought her to a circus.   There was a large tent, mostly white, but with some patched splotches of reds and blues. There were two smaller tents behind it, one for the picnic after the services and one for bathroom use. Parked behind it all a large blue bus with "Christ is King" painted on the side.

At least a hundred men, women and children dressed in their Sunday clothes milled about outside the tent waiting for the revival to begin. Lois turned to Carl. His brow was furrowed and he hit the steering wheel lightly with his open palms before returning her gaze.

"I'm sorry Lois. I've had a pretty rough time since the war. It gets really hard to talk about, but we've got a long ride home after the revival. If you'll give me another chance, I'll be glad to tell you anything you want to know."

Lois' heart twitched at his sincerity. He truly looked sorry and she knew how hard the war had been on so many men. He seemed so strong and his vulnerability towards her made her fall for him just a little easier.

"Carl, I understand. I look forward to our ride home." The dimples of her smile punctuated her interest. Grandma had called it her magic smile and she hoped it would relieve some of the tightness she saw around the corners of his mouth. She was rewarded with a smile and that duck of his head that was so endearing.

"You wait here. I'll come open your door." And he was out of the car in a flash. Coming around, he opened the door and extended his hand to help her out. She laid her hand in his, less self-conscious of his touch, more like putting her hand in her grandma's worn gardening gloves, soft and comfortable and familiar. They did not pull their hands back this time as he shut the car door and steered her toward the largest tent.

The people milling about had lined up and were being greeted at the entrance to the tent by what looked to be two matronly women who appeared to Lois to be the tallest identical twins in the world.

Maybe and Always (Maybelline and Alawin) Bannister stood at the tent opening dwarfing all those who entered. At just over six and a half feet tall, they resembled giants at a freak show rather than helpers at a tent revival. Both had iron gray hair swept up in buns. Their dresses both paisley patterned in blue hung from thin frames. Their faces were quiet pretty with sparkling blue eyes and patrician noses, although Lois definitely would have said Always was the prettier of the two.

As Carl and Lois approached the tent opening, she looked up to find that the greetings the twins were giving out like confetti had stopped abruptly. "Good evening Carl", Maybe greeted in a high sweet voice incongruous to her size, "We were under the impression that you were not going to be able to attend." And she jabbed Always in the side to confirm. Always nodded her head firmly only once, before repeating "not be able to attend".

Carl smiled broadly at them showing his "killer smile" which made each of them blush the identical color. "Ladies, I indeed thought that my duties would keep me away this evening, but God had other plans."

"Indeed." Maybe exclaimed. Both she and her sister's eyes were drawn to Carl and Lois' hands now clutched tightly together. "Who is this lovely young lady you've brought with you?" Always piped in with her identical sweet voice.

"This is Lois Cantor", he began. "You may have heard of the accident this afternoon, well it was her family that was involved. They were on their way to this very revival."

Maybe and Always shared another look before turning their eyes back to Carl so he would continue.   "Her Mama wanted her to come anyway, even with all of them lying in the hospital, and so I volunteered to bring her." He turned from their knowing looks and bowed slightly to Lois, "Miss Cantor may I introduce you to Miss Maybelline and Miss Alawin Bannister."

In the midst of the introduction Maybe and Always had begun clucking their tongues at the lost little chick in need of their care. Maybe reached out and literally enfolded Lois into her warm embrace. Always, not to be left out, came up behind Lois, hugging her and creating a cocoon of mothering.

"God's blessings child, Lord have mercy, poor, poor child." was murmured above her head.

The words seemed to surround her as the two women did. She felt an arm reach in at her shoulder and gently tug her. It was Carl freeing her from the Maybe/Always sandwich. The twins remembered themselves and drew apart allowing Lois to move back to Carl's side.

"We are so blessed you are here darling", was said in perfect twin unison, making them all laugh. "Well Carl, it should be an excellent revival. Pastor Dellaroose is in fine form!" Maybe spoke it over their heads as loud coughing and harrumphing began to swell behind them. The attendees in line, quite familiar with the twins' gift for gab, were becoming restless.

Always, who seemed the quieter of the two let her gaze followed her sister's. "Show the love of Christ people!" It was a sweetly conveyed, but a scornful look was added just in case there were any rebel rousers in their midst. Maybe put her large hand on Carl's back, smiled at Lois, and pushed them through so she and her sister could continue to greet their guests.

As they walked into the tent they waited for their eyes to adjust before locating seats in a middle row of the sea of white chairs which had been set up to face a low-rise stage.

Carl watched Lois as she walked sideways through the legs in the row they had chosen. "She looks lost", he thought and just a quickly received a stray thought, "She looks lost? How about you buddy?" He mentally pushed it away and took his seat next to Lois where she sat staring straight ahead.

"Penny for your thoughts?" Carl quietly offered leaning in close so the words reached her ears alone. She turned to face him wide-eyed and confused. She wanted to tell him she was frightened. To tell him she'd been visited by an angel and was supposed to be here. She wanted to tell him, but didn't know where to begin. Fortunately, the lantern lights in the tent were being turned up and a small country band had taken the stage.

"A Closer Walk with Thee" began to float over the audience on violin strings.

Lois began to sing, letting the words calm her spirit. Her eyes slid sideways, and she let her eyelashes hood them. Carl was still staring at her but was singing the words to the song softly under his breath. She smiled at him and him at her and in that moment, when their eyes met and their hearts opened, they connected in their spirits.

The both quickly turned their attention to the front of the tent as Pastor Dellaroose walked boldly to the podium. He was as tall and thin as the Bannister twins with a shock of white hair that waved in every direction as if greeting those present. With watery blue eyes that had seen their share of tears he took the stage as the last strains of the hymn finished playing. He looked out on his audience and then raised his head as he took his time speaking to God. He finally made a motion for the congregation to stand and in a deep but humble voice instructed, "Let us pray."

As soon as "Amen" was spoken, Maybe and Always took the stage for a passionate off-key version of Amazing Grace, before Pastor Dellaroose approached the podium with his bible in hand.

Lois noticed immediately that his demeanor had changed. He looked troubled, he looked a little afraid, and kept staring at the back of the tent as if someone had crept in. "My children, my children there is evil in this place today!"

"Amens" were heard throughout the gathering.

The pastor shook his head in apparent frustration. "I don't think you understand friends, I watched evil sneak in here today!" Suddenly, violently, he stuck his long arm out from the stage and seemed to point directly at Carl and Lois.

Maybe and Always, sitting on the stage in their appointed seats, turned their heads to look at each other and began to fan them furiously.

"Sister", the pastor continued with his finger outstretched, "I need you up on this stage please. Please!" Lois turned to look behind her and saw a man, his wife, and three small children (one picking his nose) staring at her.

She scanned the crowd behind them and saw that all eyes were on her. She didn't noticed Maybe and Always coming down from the dais and moving to either side of the row she sat in, as if to keep her from escaping.

She looked forward again at the pastor and his face had softened. "Come here little girl, it's not you who's evil, come on up." It was comical to watch every face around her relax as soon as the pastor made it known she wasn't a demon in their midst.

Lois stood almost robotically and turned to her left. She hadn't looked at Carl's face since all of this began. She couldn't. She was embarrassed and a little ashamed to have been singled out.

"I am with you, even to the end." The still small voice was like a soft breeze in the hot tent, calming her and giving her courage. Lois said "Thank you Lord."

Her feet carried her to the end of the aisle where Always was waiting. Always smiled and stuck out her hand, so Lois took it. Together in the hushed tent with all eyes on them they walked to where Pastor Dellaroose stood waiting. He took Lois' hand from Always and helped her up on to the raised stage. Lois looked up into the pastors eyes and found kindness there, and understanding.

"What's your name little lady" he asked bent toward her ear so only she could hear. This caused the audience to lean forward in unison like a wave. Each attendee hoping to hear what the pastor had whispered in the devil's ear.

Pastor Dellaroose turned to the audience suddenly shaking loose Lois' hand and throwing both of his arms outstretched toward the audience. "BE GONE In Jesus Name!!" He screamed with authority and the audience sat back in their chairs as one expelling their breath. Nervous laughter followed through the sea of the crowd.

Pastor Dellaroose pulled a linen hanky from his back pocket and wiped his face which had begun to sweat profusely. "This little girl has been in the scope of Satan for a long time." He preached, startling everyone. "She loves the Lord, but has not yet been anointed by Him and so doesn't see, doesn't understand the principalities and powers capable of taking her life!"

At least five people had stood while this scene was playing out and quietly left the tent. A few muttering about "revivals" and "didn't sign up for this." Pastor Dellaroose ignored them, ignored everything and turned his attention to Lois.

"Little girl, what brought you hear today?"

Lois was so startled by the ordeal she could not respond. She was worried that Carl would soon see the blackness, the selfishness, the corruptness in her soul; this nice pastor, quite by accident, was going to reveal every one of her sins to all those present. She stared out at the audience with dust in her throat and her tongue stuck to the roof of her mouth. Then she caught Carl's eye. He smiled at her, his soul shining through his eyes.

How did he just do that?

Not knowing and not caring, it was as if a large whoosh came out of her lungs as she said over-loudly "My Mama Angel."

This caused additional laughter from the audience, and she looked for Carl's gaze again.

When she caught it she continued, more assured now. "My Mama Angel and Papa Gus brought us, but we had an accident and they're at the hospital." She couldn't stop the sob that hiccupped past her words. Carl half-rose, prepared to rush the stage, to protect her from the hurt, but Maybe saw him and shook her head back and forth slowly. Something in her mannerism caused him to sit back down.

The pastor's long arm came around Lois and hugged her to him. "Folks", and there was an apology in his voice, "In all my years of bringing God's word to the Southwest, I've never, ever done this before, nor been asked to. But the Lord has spoken to me and I cannot ignore it. Today's revival is cancelled."

Hushed whispers began immediately, and the unshakable Maybe and Always stared at the pastor with their mouths agape.

"O.k. folks, o.k, I know you're all a bit confused. Maybe and Always here are gonna go out and ask our lovely volunteers to start the meal service a little early, so ya'll didn't come for nothing." This brought laughter but mostly from the men.

The Pastor then turned to Lois, "I need to speak in private with you and your beau...immediately!"

"No, no", Lois protested "he's not..." she never finished.

The Pastor's long arm stretched out toward Carl, crooking a finger to draw him out of his chair and up to join them on the stage.

Maybe and Always, in true servant fashion, had begun emptying the tent and directing the participants towards the picnic benches set under the smaller tent. A woman stopped, refusing to budge at the door. "I need my blessing, my son is so sick with the drink, please, pleasseeee!" she begged. Maybe looked down at the small woman in a worn dress and her face transformed to avenging angel.

"Mrs., when pastor's done with this, I promise I'll bring you in for a special anointing o.k.?"

Relief swept over the woman's face and she stood on tiptoe to kiss Maybe's cheek. "God bless you, God bless you", she croaked softly as tears streamed down her face and she walked toward the picnic area. Maybe was as confused as the visitors filing out of the congregation tent. She and her sister Always had been like sisters to the pastor. He was in fact their cousin.

Maybe and Always had been with Paul (that was his given name) since his call to serve the Lord back in the early thirties. Prior to his call, he had been a soldier, and then a farmer on his parents' farm, which was in the same town the twins' lived in. Their parents were siblings, and they saw him often at church and family gatherings. Paul called Maybe and Always to serve in 1933. Much like the Lord called His apostles.

Maybe and Always had been practical about their hopes of finding husbands in a small dusty town
who were at least as tall as them and as committed to God's work. So their original purposes for joining may have been to find their soul mates, but they had eventually stayed because they loved to see hope brought to the lives of the people they served.

The twins' parents, poor farmers struggling through the dust bowl depression, had almost felt a sense of relief when the girls had suggested they were going to do God's work with their cousin. It was a good calling, and would free up needed food resources for the girls six other siblings.

In all of this time, through many a miracle, tear, and triumph, Paul had never ever cancelled a revival!   Not when a tornado had levelled their tents. Not when flooding had washed away their first bus. Not even when he was sick with the flu that had killed so many men after the first great war. Now as Maybe stood watching Carl walk to the stage from the open door of the tent, she felt something she hadn't felt in a long time...she felt fear.

Chapter 14

The small group, which included Lois, Carl, the pastor and the twins, left the large tent and retreated to the bus parked in the back of the vacant lot.   When Lois and Carl entered they were surprised to find a quaint little home on wheels. Maybe offering to give them the grand tour, turned slowly in the front of the bus as she proudly showed off their home.

Directly to the left as you entered was a small but robust kitchen with a small dinette table which when folded down, turned into a fairly small bed. Lois smiled trying to imagine either the twins or the pastor sleeping there. Past the small kitchen were a couch and two converted rockers that were bolted to the floor. Farther down a narrow hall were bunk beds similar to beds on a train but longer, built into the left side of the bus and directly opposite them was a shower stall. Last, and a little past the beds on the left, was a commode and then Pastor Dellaroose' room which included an extra-long twin bed built into the wall, a small closet, a wash basin bolted to the floor, and a bookshelf lined with Bibles and reference guides.

They finished their tour and were led back to the sitting area. The twins sat heavily in the rockers, causing the chairs to creak in protest. The pastor invited Lois and Carl to sit on the couch which was a bright yellow sprinkled with little blue posies. After taking their seats and smiling politely at each other for a few moments, Lois cleared her throat to ask why the pastor had felt it necessary to bring her here, but the pastor interrupted before she began.

"Little lady, I am Pastor Dellaroose and I have been travelling this great country of ours for almost twenty years preaching the word of God." Perspiration leaked down his narrow face and he reached into a pocket in his coat and pulled out a handkerchief to wipe away the evidence of his anxiety.

"Never in all my days, have I actually 'seen' a demon..."

He paused for effect and was not disappointed as all four of the other occupants of the room gasped; Maybe and Always in fear, Lois in shock, and Carl in amusement. Pastor let his words sink in before continuing.

"I watched a demon walk into my tent today! Pastor Delaroose's face showed his amazement. "This demon was powerful, and he knew you, that much I could sense, but he was making me sick to my stomach and it became hard for me to concentrate because there was a tremendous buzzing in my head. Looking perplexed, he paused to scratch his ear, "It was almost like a bunch of people talking all at once, but you can't hear what any of them are saying." Maybe and Always nodded their heads furiously, enthralled by their cousin's admission.

"That is when I called you to me, for your own protection, while I banished the demon in the Lord's name. I've come up against a lot of demons sister." His eyes were now intently focused Lois, "but this one is very very bad. Just the fact that it was visible..." his voice trailed off as he relived the moment before he turned his attention to Lois once more. "Will you tell me what brought you here today?"

Lois stared back at him and tried to ease the knot that had begun to form in her stomach.

She looked in turn to the twins who were smiling patiently and then at Carl.

She had been afraid to look his way, afraid of the ridicule he'd find in this story, but when she looked into his eyes, the warmth and encouragement she saw shining back gave her new courage. She began with her grandparents, their death, her recovery, and then the words flooded out as if they would not be stopped, as if this very moment was a divine appointment for the words to be spoken. She shared her experience of living with Papa Gus and Mama Angel. She spoke about the angel's visit and what he'd said, looking at Carl and blushing when she recounted the two flesh becoming one. Last, and most difficult, was her recounting of the accident.

She described the sinister being that'd appeared in front of her, and vanished into thin air when she'd spoken the Lord's name, and how the shimmering had begun again, and she'd torn out of there terrified it was coming back. All of the words, all of the story, nothing left out, gushed out of her like a kitchen faucet. As she finished, she looked to Carl again only to find him looking at her terrified and a little green. He surprised her when he stood quietly and requested permission to go and use the facilities.

When Pastor Dellaroose replied "certainly", Carl ran down the narrow passage of the bus, threw open the door and proceeded to vomit into the commode, barely noticing the pretty rose printed wall paper it had taken Maybe and Always two weeks to finish.

Carl stood shaking in the narrow bathroom as his stomach easy from its retching. It was really just a portable toilet with a bucket underneath that could be emptied by hand. He looked in the mirror and saw his wild eyes, green complexion, and spatters of moisture caused by the vomit on his patrol uniform.

"Can this be real?" His mind was spinning. His thoughts twisted like a tornado, like a cyclone tearing up memories and spinning them around at random. Was it possible that Lois knew? Was it possible she was some kind of government spy sent to see if he had talked? It all seemed so insane, and yet his spirit had connected with hers, and he'd felt it like a low electric hum when they'd held hands.

A prayer started in his heart as he wedged himself into the commode, wondering how either the twins or the pastor went to the restroom in private. "Lord, I am a simple man, thrown into extraordinary circumstances; please I need your guidance." As he finished he opened his eyes and looked at himself in the small shaving mirror over the commode. His color was better, but his eyes were still a little wild. He rubbed his hands over his face to erase the fear that kept welling and settling in his stomach.

He began to feel confined, boxed in, it was the same exact feeling he'd had on D-Day, when he and his lieutenant squeezed into a bunker the size of a bunny hole and lay for 6 hours under heavy fire. At different points, he and his lieutenant had both had to keep each other from jumping up firing a spray of bullets and hoping the enemy would hit them and put them out of their misery. It's where he'd learned to pray. It's where he'd learned there was a God.

Now it seemed he'd been thrown into something he was totally unprepared for. As he stood wiping the spittle from his uniform, he made decision. He would go out, excuse himself, let them know this wasn't his battle and tell them he had to get back to work. At that precise moment a hand landed on his shoulder.

He looked up into the mirror to see who had come in and was astonished to find the bathroom had become a palatial entryway. A crowd of beings stood looking off a veranda with their arms lifted as they sang in voices that made Carl weep before he knew the tears were streaming from his eyes.

The beings were giving glory to God in the highest! And the hand on his shoulder allowed him to fall to his knees and begin to worship with them, but just for a moment. The gentle hand then lifted him to his feet with just the slightest pressure.

He looked in the mirror, afraid to turn around, and saw...CHRIST...was that Jesus Christ standing behind him, holding his shoulder and loving him? Loving him so much that his shame at standing before his God was too much and he wailed out his hurt and fear.

Jesus used his own hand to wipe away the tears from Carl's eyes.

Christ's eyes were like fire, beautiful and clean and knowing. He spoke to Carl softly, but the words were large in his heart. "You've seen, you know, you are chosen, fulfill your purpose." And then Christ gave him a gift; An image of he and Lois now old, sitting on a porch on a beautiful farm laughing and having a glass of "hoity-toity" wine. It was beautiful and perfect and Carl fell to his knees again thanking the Lord for something he could not even conceive.

Just as he finished his "amen" and looked up, he was back in the bathroom and the wallpaper was all that stared back at him. He almost tried to scratch it away. To bring back the vision, to bring back Christ, but then he felt Him, in his heart, in his soul, and he was at peace.

Out in the sitting area, the pastor, the twins and Lois heard Carl vomiting, then praying, then silence. "I think I'll just go check on him and make sure he's alright." Lois was out of her seat before anyone could protest. Just as she reached the twins sleeping area, the accordion door of the commode area was flung open. Lois' hand flew to her chest and she stepped back in surprise.

Carl marched out of the small room like he was going to war. He looked at Lois and for just a moment she saw heaven in the glow from his countenance, before gasping at the single flame ignited on his forehead, and like a silly school girl, she fainted dead away.

When she revived, she was lying on the little yellow sofa with the blue posies, and her head was aching. She looked with some confusion at all the faces towering over her with concern. She started to ask what had happened, when the events that led up to her fainting spell flashed quickly through her mind, and her eyes sought out Carl. He stood to her left, his face closest to hers and she looked quickly to his forehead…nothing. No flame, no luminescence in his face, and her hand shot out before she had time to consider it, tentatively touching the place where the flame had been. As she rubbed the spot on his forehead, he smiled, grabbed her hand and kissed it before God and a pastor no less!

Lois was confused though her headache was getting better and she sat up gently pulling her hand from Carl's.

"Carl are you alright? What happened in that bathroom?"

Before he could speak, Pastor Dellaroose suggested everyone resume their seats so Carl could explain. Carl marched over and sat so close to Lois, she had to scooch over just so her leg wasn't pinned under his.

The pastor resumed his seat next to Lois on the other side of the couch. He looked at the two young people with kind eyes and opened his mouth ready to continue his lecture about the demon following them, when Carl stood and with no preemptive build up, began to speak.

"Pastor, Lois, ladies (a wink and a nod), I believe I may have some information pertinent to this situation. Until five minutes ago, I would have said that demons don't exist, and that God helps those who help themselves, but I've been changed! In a commode no less!" Then he began to laugh. Only a chuckle at first, and then building to that deep rumble that made Lois' knees bend, just a little.

Soon they were all laughing heartily, as if drops of joy had been sprinkled on the breeze floating in through the yellow and white polka dot curtains that decorated each of the buses twenty odd windows. As the laughter became chuckles again, each face looked at Carl expectantly waiting for him to share his transforming experience.

"Christ Himself just told me what His purpose is for me!" Carl smiled widely as his voice picked up steam. "He showed me I don't need to be afraid or uncertain, that He will wipe away every one of my tears!" At this his eyes welled up ready to prove his point, but he laughed through them. "I need to share with you all something that happened three summers ago..."

Chapter 15

July 1, 1948 Roswell, NM

Carl was 23 years old when he left the Army.

He had landed shore duty as a base medic just a few hours from his home town of Albuquerque, New Mexico at the Roswell Army Airfield, reporting to his Lieutenant (now a Captain), who had started his military career as a fighter pilot.

It was the first of July and it was hot. He'd been home to see his family (Mom, Aunt, and three sisters) just the week before, and was glad to see their farm was holding strong.

He was on the last stretch of his enlistment. Two more months and he'd be able to move back home and help out. Today however, he was on duty filing medical reports, answering calls, and taking a smoke break when he could. He'd just lit up his Camel non-filter when the jeep he had his foot hiked up on began to quiver and shake.

Carl dropped his cigarette, stepped on it and turned in a three hundred and sixty degree circle trying to find the cause for the shaking. Men were running from different areas of the airfield, some of them starting to point up. Carl joined them just in time to see two large spherical objects "pop" through the air, as if they had appeared by magic, then move like lightning across the sky and blink out of sight with a bright light and shimmering heat. The men who had joined Carl on the airfield stood staring not saying a word, shocked and terrified.

Carl finally shook himself out of his stupor and began running towards his captain's office. The movement seemed to free his brothers in arms from their stupor and they began running towards their planes, ready to get up and find out what the heck had just invaded their airspace.   As Carl reached the Captain's doorway he pulled up short and watched him on the telephone yelling obscenities and telling his command that two unidentified objects had just invaded American airspace.

After several hours and at least eight fly-bys of their planes, it was concluded that a sun-spot phenomena had occurred causing the base to experience a mass-hallucination.   Carl ate it up. He could not explain what he'd seen, nor did he want to. He just wanted to finish his tour and get home.

***

Approximately five days later, while Carl was sleeping in his barracks, he felt a rough hand shake him awake at three in the morning. "Wedner, Wedner!" the hand was that of his Captain.

"Get up Wedner, we've got to go out to the Foster Ranch, get up!"

Carl shook off the sleep that clung to him as he hurriedly dressed in his uniform. "What is it Captain, what's wrong?" His Captain looked older in the filtered moonlight creeping into the window above the bunk beds.

Captain J.L Morgan was not a man given to flights of fancy. He'd seen enough of war and death, but knew his life would never be the same after this night. There was no one else who could help him get through it except Carl Wedner.

"Son." His voice was harsh and excited at the same time. "This will be the most important mission of our lifetime I have no doubt. That mass hallucination we all witnessed...it just crash landed outside Roswell near the Foster's ranch!" His Captain's words woke him like no cold water bath ever could and Carl was immediately on high alert.

"What are we waiting for Captain", he said flashing his wicked grin, "let's go."

***

A convoy of jeeps and military vehicles wound its way through the darkness, lit only by the light of the stars and the headlamps on the cars. From above they looked like a small glowing worm snaking around turns on rough terrain.

The base command's General led the detail. His jeep, at the head of the convoy, stopped at the gate to the Foster ranch. The General moved with agility as he exited the passenger side and went and stood next to a man tucked safely on the other side of the gate. The man, who appeared to work on the ranch, as evidenced by his shadowed overalls and straw hat was waving his arms wildly and pointing north. The General grabbed hold of the man's shoulder's and shook him slightly. This seemed to calm him.

After a few more minutes of conversation the General patted the man on the back a couple times, waved, and climbed back into the jeep. His arm came up in a forward motion and they were driving again. Carl looked at his Captain sitting next to him two jeeps back from the front.

"Hey Cap, you're not buying any of this are you?" His question was flippant. He hoped it would lighten the mood that had enshrouded the snaking worm like a cocoon.

His Captain looked him directly in the eye before answering, "We'll know soon enough son, we'll know soon enough."

Carl with infinitesimal hesitation put the vehicle into gear and began following at a safe distance from the jeeps in front of him. It was a long trip, several hours, and Carl's head was beginning to ache from the dust and fumes created by the train of cars headed out into the desert night. He adjusted his rump and was just about to ask if they were getting close when the General's jeep screeched to a halt just as it crested a slight rise a thousand feet ahead of them.

"Whoas" could be heard as the cars struggled to stop before creating a collision. The occupants of each of the open topped vehicles either whispered low or stood in their seats, gaping.

The General, looking like some kind of shadowed demon warrior, stood outlined by an orange silvery haze that spread across the landscape just past the crest of the hill. He motioned for his leadership with his hand without turning around.

"Come on Carl, that means you too." his Captain said sharply causing Carl to jump from the vehicle double-time. He walked briskly with his Captain until they were standing on what Carl could only imagine in his mind as the brink of hell. Carnage like none of them had ever seen before lay like a gaping red hot wound before them.

Half buried in dirt and glass created by the impact, lay two disc shaped objects burning bright hot yellow and orange. Debris littered the ground three football fields long in front of them.   And then they saw movement.

The General signaled the troops to fan out along the ridge. The boots, who were trained to do as they were ordered, complied, but fear was outlined in the profiles of their faces. The new grunts held their guns with shaking hands ready to fire. What were those things down there? They definitely weren't human...each man stood his ground, but just barely.

There were approximately six beings below them walking around in the debris; tall and thin with no clothing, their heads abnormally large. Further detail was difficult to ascertain from their current positions.   Gender from their vantage point was undeterminable.

The General, who had a scowl on his face, had been promoted for his brutality during the war. He relished a good fight, and raised his arm as if to commence firing...until one of the beings who'd been looking at the damage to its ship turned and gazed directly at him. The General's jaw instantaneously went slack, and a small amount of spittle crept out of the corner of his mouth.

He motioned to Carl's captain and a few lieutenants to follow him down, telling the rest of the troops to "hold fast"...and "that was an order!"   The Captain turned to Carl and said "follow me."

Carl wanted to tell him to go to hell, he wanted to say "I didn't sign up for this", but instead he found his feet following the greeting party down the hill. As they approached the wreckage, Carl noticed a heavy odor of sulfur, and the bodies. There were approximately twenty to thirty beings scattered all over the crash site.   They appeared to be dead, which was only evidenced by the fact that they continued to lay on the ground and the familiar motion of a rising and falling chest was absent.

The being, which had looked at the General while he stood on the ridge, walked over and stood in front of him. Its hands, attached to over-long arms, had six digits. It raised its right arm, in an eerily similar salute most of the men standing there recognized as that used by the Nazis.

The General jaw continued to hand slack, but this time so was everyone else in the group...everyone except for Carl.

Carl burned with fury, but he could not say why, until the being looked directly at him. Evil, liar, deceiver, all of these thoughts came to Carl's mind when that...that...thing looked at him,   Not with soulless eyes, but eyes that harbored a soul so depraved and rotten that it made the hairs on Carl's neck stand up.

The being appeared to sense something equally foul in him, because he somehow communicated to the General that Carl needed to leave. His Captain looked at him with empty eyes and a slack-jaw while stuttering haltingly, "Go back to the jeep and wait for us there."
Carl tried to argue, but his Captain had already turned his head back to the being as if he were listening to a conversation. Carl spat on the ground near the being's feet before turning and running back up the hill.

Roswell Revival, 1950

As Carl finished his story and looked expectantly at each of the faces gathered round him, he expected to see shock, or horror, or disbelief, but all that stared back was fear.

Pastor Dellaroose spoke first. "I read the papers about the incident, and quite frankly thought it was a bunch of hog-wash. Apparently, I was very wrong." The Pastor seemed to be considering his next question carefully.

"Did your Captain or anyone that was there tell you what this being shared with them?" Carl looked drained and wild eyed as he responded. "Ya...ya, my captain told me, it's when I decided to leave the military service.

***

The group that went down the hill was gone for about an hour. Then they all started climbing back up the hill. Certain men were chosen to work as the clean- up detail, and one of the transport trucks was commandeered to bring the beings back to the base.

When my captain made it back to our jeep, he seemed different, like it wasn't him anymore.

He was almost evangelical when he turned to me and shared what had transpired, like he wanted me to believe."

He said, "Carl, these beings are an ancient alien race. They've been watching us for thousands of years, waiting for the right moment to come and help us evolve to the beings we are supposed to be. They've lived here before; were worshipped by ancient civilizations as gods, but had to leave because our minds could not sustain the knowledge they were trying to share. They are going to open doors to things we've only ever read about in science fiction. They are going to make us gods!"

Carl slowly shook his head back and forth, and his hands had begun to tremble. He looked at the group sitting in this old bus, and the incongruity of the situation made his whole body quake a large shiver.

"They took at least eighteen of those things back to the base. Stories of two bodies found dead, or one being alive were lies." This time Carl looked at Lois. If she thought he was crazy, he probably wouldn't be able to bear it. He was surprised but happy to see she wasn't staring at him as if he'd lost his mind. She did look however very, very sad.

"I think those things killed my grandparents." Her hands busily wiping away tears as she said it. "I saw the shimmering, and the lightning scrolling up the sky. Lois' voice caught on the memory before she continued. "I watched the burning heat destroy everything I loved."

Carl's arm went around her slowly, but instinctively, and she leaned into him just as intuitively.

Pastor Dellaroose stood abruptly. "God is my rock and my salvation, whom shall I fear!" he quoted, before looking at Carl and Lois huddled on the couch. "I need to fast and pray, I suggest we all do the same tonight and meet back here in the morning."

Each of them understood that supernatural barriers had been breached. Knew that for some reason, they were involved, and felt the order to fast and pray resound in their spirits like a harmony. Carl stood with Lois' hand in his, shook the pastor's with his other, and flashed his wicked grin to the twins.

"How does ten a.m. sound?"

***

Carl and Lois were quiet in the glow of the car's lighted dashboard. In unison their eyes scanned the now empty field where a revival occurred, but not the one they'd been expecting. The sun had set, but the breeze was still warm.

Lois looked sideways at Carl praying silently for courage to ask him about the night he saw what he did. Finally, she cleared her throat just a little, filling the patrol car with noise, making Carl take his eyes from the road for just a moment.

"Are you o.k.?" His question was laced with concern.

She smiled in the darkness of the car. He was so sweet, so attentive, so...so...so sure of himself. Lois envied that. "I...I just wanted to know what your thoughts were about my visit from an angel, my grandparents death, and your own experience with these...things!"

Carl was a conscientious man, particularly when he drove. He didn't take his eyes from in front of him, but he did take his hand off the two o'clock and reach for hers across the leather seat.

"You know I believe Christ is the son of God and our way to heaven.", he replied quietly, focusing on the road as he spoke, not used to sharing something so personal with someone he barely knew, even if he liked her...a lot. She looked at him kindly and his smile said he was trying. "If I was a betting man, I'd say they were evil, whatever they were, which means they aren't from God." His explanation so well stated without inserting hyperbole, or puffing up his role in the whole thing, soothed Lois like a balm.

Before she could comment on his words he said, "Now I have a question for you if that's alright?" At her nod of consent he pushed forward, turning a bright red to the tips of his ears,

"You mentioned that the angel you saw said you would meet a 'partner', here he stuttered just a bit "...do...is there...is it possible..."

Lois smiled secretly to herself as she watched him struggle to get the words out, and then felt sorry for him and finished his sentence for him.

"Do I think you might be him?" Her eyes stared straight ahead.

He seemed relieved he didn't have to finish the sentence himself. "Yes, that's what I'm asking Lois."

Funny thing was Lois wasn't sure herself. She'd only just met Carl, but things did appear to be leading in that direction. It brought to mind the war; the crazy marriages almost daily in the newspaper, at their local churches, and the justice of the peace. It had seemed so romantic to a girl of thirteen. Not all of them had lasted, but some had. It was becoming clear to her that she was in a war of some kind. An enemy had killed her loved ones, hurt them, and now was determined to what? Kill her as well? She turned her gaze back to Carl in the dark of the police cruiser's cab.

"Carl, I...I must confess, I truly don't know. I'm confused and scared and worried and battered. I've spent the last few years just trying to begin life again after what happened to my grandparents." The car slowed as she spoke. Carl quietly pulled over to the side of the road and turned to Lois encouraging her to continue with his smile.   She bent her head and continued.

"Now, my adopted family is lying in the hospital. I'm afraid to care about someone, I'm afraid to be obedient to God. I'm afraid this is all leading to something I can't handle, and I'm really not prepared to drag someone new into it."

Carl had watched Lois, more than listened, but the meaning came across in the hurt and fear on her face. He understood the confusion and fear. He himself felt that he was living in some kind of bubble that only existed when they were together. It made him feel fuzzy and confused, but when he was with her, and it was happening, it was all as clear as a bell. His faith may have been   "Man   Upstairs"   faith,   but   the 'coincidences' of their hurried relationship were speaking to a part of him he'd never acknowledged.

In the past he'd managed to bury experiences like the one in the desert; the war, his father leaving them to "follow his dream", poverty, along with other life events that had wounded or scarred or haunted him. As he sat next to her now however, he wanted to dig it up and let her see it, and see understanding, or at least acceptance, in her eyes.

"I know you're afraid, Lois. I'm afraid too, but I'd rather be afraid with you, and that's never happened to me before."
His words seemed to open up a flood of emotion in Lois as she stared at this stranger she'd just met, but couldn't imagine not seeing again. Fear, hope, anxiety, excitement, they streamed through her all at once like a concerto making

her feel light headed and dizzy. She put her hands to her temples rubbing them, and coming to a decision, began to nod her head slowly before speaking again.

"You'll need to be introduced to my family, and we'll need to get to know each other, but I do believe you are who the angel spoke to me about." There. She'd said it.

Carl whooped loudly as they approached the hospital and Lois giggled next to him.

***

After arriving at the hospital and checking in on the children and Papa Gus, who were all resting comfortably, Lois left Carl in the room the hospital had given her for the length of her family's stay and went to see Mama Angel. She found her reclining slightly in her hospital bed, awake, but fuzzy from the morphine she'd been given.

As soon as she saw Lois, tears filled in her good eye. "Oh Niña, are you all right? I've been so worried about what was going to happen at that revival. Satan has tried everything he can to hurt you, my poor baby."

Lois almost...almost laughed. Leave it to Mama to worry about her when she was lying in a hospital bed with one eye missing! "Mama, I'm fine and I've so much to tell you but first I want to let you know I've contacted the hospital in Albuquerque and they are arranging transportation for the whole family to be taken nearer to home."

Mama Angel's good eye looked surprised and pleased. "Thank you Niña, thank you. How are the babies? I tried to go see them but the nuns here are like Nazi's and they insist I can't get out of bed." Lois recounted everyone's condition and then came to the heart of the reason she was there, besides reassuring herself her Mama was o.k.

Perched on the edge of a chair next to the bed, she leaned close to her Mama's ear. "I believe I've met the man that the angel spoke to me about, and I believe we have a small piece of the puzzle as to why we had to be here…She took a deep breath …but in order to find out what all this is about I'm going to have to stay here for a time and work with him to find God's purpose in this." She cringed expectantly as she said the last part because she knew Mama Angel would be upset she was going to be so far away.

As usual, Mama surprised Lois and smiled from ear to ear stretching the bandages, until a few came loose. "Praise Jesus, praise Him! I have prayed for a man for you since you came to stay with us! My prayers are answered!"

Lois sat back in the chair, shocked (and a little hurt), by Mama Angel's reaction.

Seeing her words had upset Lois, Angela reached out her right hand over the railings of the bed. Lois took it in hers.

"Niña, I've known since you were a young girl, since you first came to stay with us…no no even before then in the hospital, that God had a purpose and plan for you much bigger than my own. This is where you belong for now, and it's exciting!"

Lois leaned in conspiratorially. "It's Carl! The policeman who helped us get to the hospital, he's the one the angel spoke about! I just know it!"

Mama Angel nodded wisely. "Isn't it funny how the Lord works?" Bafflement edged her voice as her good eye began to droop. Lois could see she'd worn her out. She stood and leaned over the bed to kiss her goodnight.

"I'm going back…Carl and I are going back to meet with Pastor Dellaroose in the morning to see if we can figure out what we need to do next. I'll come and see you when we get back and fill you in o.k.?"

Mama's head nodded slowly. Her last piece of advice before drifting off was "Remember the Lord will reveal it to you, just ask."

Chapter 16

NE – Wedner Farm 2001

The shadows of her memories brushed against her like children seeking attention. They were painful but also exciting and she missed Carl and his confidence and his wicked smile.

The Beloved family sat back collectively rubbing their eyes, or taking a deep breath. Pastor Wallen, who'd arrived quietly, excused himself to use the restroom.

Lois had been sharing her story for almost eight hours but she wasn't done. Not yet.

"Carl and I learned more than we ever wanted to know about evil and this world. We spent forty years of our fifty year marriage fighting principalities and powers that most people have never conceived of, but we also learned, very well, how to listen to our still small voice." The seriousness of her statement was dispelled when she stood and moved to the kitchen. "Anyone hungry?"

***

Once again the Beloved's, Lois, and Pastor Wallen sat around the dining room table replete and full. "Who's going to help with the dishes?" Lois wanted to know.

Pastor Wallen burped, turned red, and stood from the table. He explained that he had to get to the church for a counselling session. "I'll leave your folks to finish."

Chris and Sara both jumped up without fighting or arguing and began to clear dishes as Pastor Wallen exited through the front door. John and Annie glanced at each other and with eyebrows raised looked back to Lois.

"Lois" John felt like he was forever explaining why they had to leave. "Are we getting close to how this all ties in with our family and this trip? I really believe if we don't get on the road tonight or at the very latest tomorrow morning, we are going to end up spending this vacation in Nebraska."

Lois laughed at John's not so subtle question. "John I think we are very close and I would like to beg your indulgence one more time." Lois broke off her explanation as Chris and Sara came back through the swinging door, picking up dishes and going back into the kitchen.

Lois, John, and Annie watched them go before Lois leaned forward and lowered her voice.

"I can finish my story tonight, and I think I need to. I believe the Random and his soldiers know you are here and staying any longer could become dangerous to everyone."

John sat back drawing Annie with him, concern and not a little fear showing in their eyes. "Are you telling me my family and I are being chased by aliens?" His voice echoed the absurdity of the question. Lois didn't laugh. She looked John in the eye and grabbed his hand before replying.

"John, they are alien to us, but these are not flying saucer, beam me up, beings. They are so beyond our mortal understanding of evil, so focused on their purpose to destroy, so without any moral compass, that we cannot even put them into a context or reference source."

Now Annie sat forward but cocked her ear toward the kitchen. She could hear Chris and Sara laughing and dishes clinking and turned her attention back to the huddled group.

"So you're saying they're demons?"

Lois wasn't sure how to explain all the things she'd learned over a lifetime in such a short period of time, but she knew it had to be done tonight. A thought struck her and she jumped spryly out of her seat and headed for the stairs before remembering her guests. She glanced back over her shoulder, "Come on, I have something to show you." Annie and John were out of their seats immediately.

John headed for the stairs but Annie stuck her index finger in the air requesting a pause as she moved to the swinging door. Popping her head inside the kitchen, she giggled out loud as she watched Chris and Sara work like an Olympic Dish Team.

"Hey" she said suddenly, making them both jump and turn around. "Your father and I are going upstairs with Lois for a few minutes. When you're finished you can go in the parlor and watch TV. until we come down."

Sara looked at her mom and smiled. "So were staying again?" Chris nodded his agreement with the assumption.

"We'll see." was all Annie would commit to before turning to disappearing through the door to find Lois and John. She found them upstairs in the hallway. Lois turned toward them then looked up. Above her head was a rope attached to a pull-down stairwell to her attic.

"I've saved several journals and some video of Carl's and my 'ministry'. I should have thought of it earlier but I think you needed to hear the 'bones' of the story first anyway, or it might all just have seemed like gibberish." She finished her speech while reaching for the pull that brought the stairs down so they could continue their discussion in the attic.

The attic, like the rest of Lois' house was quaint. Partially finished, it was neatly piled with memories marked on boxes and seen in souvenirs and furniture spread around the room. Lois, in her fastidious fashion, walked to a back corner of the attic where a large sea chest sat alone.

John and Annie came and stood behind her peeking over her shoulder as she bent down and opened the latches. "Please don't be alarmed by what I am about to show you. I think it will stun you more than anything, but I have found that most people just want to ignore this."   Lois gave an apologetic smile over her shoulder as she said it.

John and Annie, who were living in a perpetual state of shock at this point just shrugged their shoulders and waited to see the contents. The opening of the lid of the trunk was a little anti-climactic as the first thing anyone looked at was a large wedding dress, beautifully embroidered, but yellowed with age. Lois looked over her shoulder again, blushing this time.

"Oops, this is a relic! My wedding dress. It actually belonged to Maybe and Always. They only bought one and planned on sharing it if either of them ever got married!" This statement brought a much needed laugh break before they got down to business.

Lois carefully removed the gown and set it on boxes next to the trunk. She continued to remove other odds and ends before letting John and Annie know she'd found what she was looking for with an "ah ha!" Waving her hand behind her, to let them know to back up, she began dragging the trunk into the middle of the room to let some light into the contents of the trunk.

At first, neither John nor Annie, were particularly impressed by what they were seeing. Piles of magazines from SPY to the National Inquirer sat atop the other contents creating a line of sight barrier at least three inches thick. Lois removed these as carefully as the dress, which caused John and Annie to look at each other and smirk. Once they were removed however, Annie and John both gasped in amazement…and fear.

***

Chris and Sara were just finishing up the dishes when they heard the scratching. They almost missed it at first because they'd been having an unusually good time together. It had been like this when they were young and had lived in a rural area of San Diego County in the city of Julian. With only each other to play with, they'd become best pals for a while.

Chris heard it first; scratching on the walls outside the kitchen, loud, like the timbers of the house were being breached. Chris turned to Sara ready to grab her hand when he saw her staring out the window into the night. All that stared back were soulless eyes large and unblinking.

Outside of Time
The old thing. Wrinkled and shriveled. She is spent.

The lesser in these circles are terrified of her. She'd been given 'the gifts'. Not just a gift, but each of them.   It did indeed make her a formidable foe, but as has been learned in these circles, and had been sung so well by the Rolling Stones...time is on our side.

The girl is mine to destroy! A Masterpiece in time! The old woman, the 'thorn in the side' if you will, was a bonus.

***

Soulless eyes, large and unblinking stared from piles and piles of photos in the next section of the chest. As John and Annie began to sift through the dozens and dozens of photos their horror grew. Pictures of these satanic beings in fires, earthquakes, car accidents, war scenes, brothels, bridge collapses, and the list went on. Soccer game stampedes, serial killers, pedophiles.

The pictures did not readily give up their information, but Lois (or Carl) had taken the time to circle in red felt pen a being or beings recognizable by a smeared face in a cloud or hidden in a morning crowd.

John and Annie were so overcome with the evidence presented to them, that Lois was the first to hear the screaming. She was at the stairs to the attic before she realized that John and Annie were not following her. "John...Annie!" she screamed.

John and Annie looked up as one and moved the same way as they heard their children screaming in terror from the kitchen. Within seconds they were in the kitchen swinging the door wide as all three entered like soldiers.

Once again, life went into 'pretend' mode. It was as if God had given them the mind of Christ because everything in the kitchen felt more 'real'. The intensity was like the pressure you feel in an airplane, but had the effect of sharply focusing each of them.

Chris stood in front of Sara who was crouched behind his legs with her back to the cupboard under the sink. To his right near the stove stood the being who had followed them; the one that had tried to kill Sara and Annie.

John acted on his first impulse and rushed toward the being to...he didn't know what...take him down...kill it...He was stopped when the being turned toward him. Those eyes, those eyes...they began to tell him things before he'd taken two steps. The demon showed him in pictures, devoid of hope, what his plans were for his family, but he didn't just show him, he pressed it into his mind as if it had already happened. John fell to his knees crying and praying "help me Lord", and shaking his head furiously to get rid of the images.

The evil thing began a slow turn back toward Chris and Sara, but Lois had had enough...and in her home with her guests no less!

Lois couldn't have shocked those in the kitchen more as she began to sing. "Jesus loves me, yes he does, Jesus loves me yes he does".

The being twisted its head toward Lois, completing a two hundred and seventy degree turn on its thin stick neck and hissed. Not out loud, but everyone in the room heard it and it sounded like acid being dropped on their eardrums, as if they could actually hear the pain.

Lois' knees bent in and she almost dropped to the floor from the pain in her head, but she stood again and began to recite Psalm twelve. Random watched from his viewpoint near the stove.

The old thing is weak, he could smell it. If he could stand the pain of His name just a little longer…Lois felt the nausea building. She knew this was always bad, it always started this way.

A standoff was in the making, and Lois for her part was terrified that she was too old, and that this would be the time the Random would win. Just as she fell to her knees squeaking out Christ's name over and over again the kitchen was illuminated by a brilliant light. Lois lifted her hand to protect her eyes and looked up. Her soul rejoiced at what she saw.

John and Annie had moved toward the children as the Random continued its battle with Lois.
They now stood hand in hand with their children, their backs all up against the counter in a line. The flame on Sarah's head burned like a beacon as she recited the Lord's Prayer. As her voice grew in strength, she was joined by her brother, father and mother as they too began to recite the twenty-third Psalm.

Growls of frustration from a rabid dog began to fill their heads as they continued their assault. Annie and John winced in pain and had to refocus several times to continue. Chris allowed tears of pain to fall from his eyes without wiping them. But Sara…Sara, Lois could see, looked like a warrior as she began to speak the Word.

Sara was angry!   Angry that this thing had ruined a perfectly good evening. Angry that this THING had the audacity to hurt her family. And angry that her new friend, this wonderful woman who had opened her home to her family when they were in trouble, was bent over in pain.

She reached into herself, she searched her inner heart, and she found waiting quietly, patiently, her Lord and Savior ready to do battle, it made Sara laugh out loud with His joy.

Random was no stranger to the maniacal giggles induced by the avenger. Time was of the essence. He reached behind his back and pulled out a wicked blade that dripped with distain and hatred, as if it too was alive. He staggered toward the Beloveds raising his arm as he did so.

Sara, in the throws' of her own Holy Ghost revival, reached out her hand just as Random brought the blade down and cried out "JESUS LIVES IN ME!"

The screech from Random was in perfect harmony to the downward thrust of its blade. It caught Sara's hand and glanced off with a shower of the illuminating light glowing from her body, but not before slicing cleanly through her pinky finger and severing it from her hand.

Sara felt nothing. She did not even appear to notice she'd just lost an appendage. She continued her barrage of the Word, knowing innately that IT was the weapon, and that no weapon formed against the Word could stand.

Random screamed his frustration! Returning again to his master without their heads was not an option. Careful after millennia, knowing that timing was everything.   Random screeching blasphemies in each of their heads, shimmered, and disappeared from the kitchen.

His parting words hung in the air like icicles; "You are next old bag of bones!"

Lois took stock of the situation from her place on the floor as the Beloved's rushed to Sara who was bleeding profusely from her missing appendage. She watched Chris look around on the floor for the missing finger, and finding it, rush to the sink to wash it.

Lois grasped the edge of the counter above her, holding out her hand to Chris, and admonishing him not to wash it. Shaking herself, she moved quickly to the sink area.

Annie had wrapped Sara's hand in a dishtowel and was applying pressure and hugging Sara to her. Lois took Sara's digit from Chris before commanding, "Pray with me, all of you!" She bent down stealing Sara's hand away from Annie who struggled to hold on. Lois looked her directly in the eye, "Trust me!" She said it with such conviction that Annie immediately loosened her grip. Lois unwrapped the towel and laid Sara's pinky finger inside near where it was missing from the young girls hand, rewrapped it and bowed her head.

"Father, we ask for your intervention and healing Father. We see a road we are all prepared to follow and pray for wholeness prior to our beginning. You are our light and our salvation, whom shall we fear! We thank you Father, in Jesus name." With shaky hands, Lois again slowly unwrapped the towel from Sara's hand.

To say the Beloved's were amazed would have been an understatement. Nestled in the bloody towel, Sara's hand lay…whole! Her pinky finger wriggled as if to prove it.

Lois did not allow them to marvel for long. "Beloved family we are in perilous danger!" All heads turned from gawking at Sara's hand to Lois.

"The Random will be back. I need to finish telling you the truth before his return which should be about a day. You've wounded it Sara, but it will not stop until we are all dead." The Beloveds stood as a family and all eyes focused on John. The Random had made a mistake. It was apparent in John's eyes.

Righteous indignation showed in his face and trembled from every muscle in his body as he brought his emotions under control. That thing, that monster, had hurt his baby! He looked at each of his family members in turn starting with Annie. She gave a slight affirmative nod reading the purpose in his gaze. Chris did the same, looking so much like a man that John's eyes teared up with pride. He looked last at his baby girl who was stretching her hand and wiggling her finger in disbelief. When she looked at her father, and he recognized the resolve in her eyes, he let the tears loose. Turning to the diminutive warrior he nodded and said, "We're in!"

***

The Beloved family stood united in the attic. Lois had stayed behind to lock up the house and now she clambered up the stairs. She came in directing everyone to sit on the floor. They all did as they were instructed finding seats around the trunk in the middle of the room. Pictures and magazines were scattered everywhere. As the Beloved's sifted through the pictures, Lois continued to rummage. She let out a triumphant "Aha!" and sat back drawing everyone's attention.

What they saw was a leather bound book stamped with the initials "LW". Lois surprisingly remained silent as she stared at the book. Her life was here in these pages. Memories, good and bad, all scribed in ink on yellowed pages. She looked up and smiled, just a little. "Are you all ready to hear the truth?"

Her look and tone made each of the Beloveds silently question whether they were ready or not. John took the initiative. "I don't think we really have a choice in this..." Before he could finish Lois interrupted, "Every human being has a choice John. It is what separates us from the animals, and the evil. You all have the choice to decide to finish this, or walk away."

"But what would happen to us if we walk away?" he wanted to know. "Wouldn't we all be killed anyway?"

Lois shrugged her shoulders. "I really couldn't tell you, but I know that one of the greatest gifts we've ever received has been our sovereign free will."

All eyes were on John as he shook his head back and forth chuckling to himself. "I guess we either have to trust the Lord and surrender our wills to Him, and face the unknown, or leave and trust in ourselves to face it."

As John finished speaking, he thought wistfully of his life just three days prior. He only allowed himself a moment. He would not look back; he would not follow Lot's wife down that road. His hand went out flat in front of him creating a spoke to the wheel they'd created around the trunk.

"Beloveds, Lois, let's do this!" Each of them starting with Annie and ending with Lois stuck their hands; out finishing the wheel. Lois, eyes twinkling, felt the rush of excitement that had lain dormant in her for thirty years, "Get ready Beloveds! We're going on an adventure!"

Chapter 17

Tent Revival Location, Roswell NM 1950

Carl and Lois arrived at the Pastor's bus at seven am. They could see that they would not have to worry about waking the Pastor or the twins. Each was outside the bus overseeing some part of the day's revival program. They walked quickly toward the pastor waving to Maybe and Always as they passed by.

"Pastor we're here." Carl waved; a 'cat ate the canary' look on his face.

Pastor Dellaroose turned at the sound of his name. He watched as Carl and Lois closed the gap between them with a look of concern on his face. "How would he tell them about his dream last night? Were these young people prepared for what was ahead?" The Lord covered his unease like a balm. "Be still and know that I am God" resonated inside him.

He plastered a smile on his face and stuck out his hand to greet Carl and Lois. "Good morning!" the pastor nearly shouted, startling the couple. Carl and Lois responded with their own hello before Pastor Dellaroose suggested they return to the bus to continue their discussion from the night before.

He signaled to the twins who'd secretly been observing the conversation. After leaving their orders with their respective helpers, they moved toward the bus softly singing a hymn. When they entered Carl and Lois were seated on the little couch with their heads bowed while the pastor stood over them praying for strength, mercy, grace, and perseverance. The twins immediately bowed their heads and joined in the prayer. After the closing 'amen', the twins moved to their rocking chairs and the pastor took a seat on the couch next to the couple.

Pastor Dellaroose gave each of them a hard stare before he spoke. "I've had a dream." His voice, soft and caring, was a direct contradiction to the stare they'd just received. As he shared his vision, Maybe and Always, who'd been told about the pastor's dream, had begun to quietly pray in unison.

"The things that I am about to tell you are directly from the Lord. I know it may sound crazy, but I believe...no I know that to ignore my dream will mean danger to you both."

Carl and Lois, who had come to an understanding that they must commit the rest of their lives to each other in order to follow the plan the Lord had for them, couldn't imagine anything stranger.

The pastor stood and began pacing the length of the space between either sides of the bus.

"I'm not sure how else to tell you this..." here he hesitated again, "I need to marry you right now!"

Pastor Dellaroose was quite discomfited as Carl and Lois began first to giggle, and then laugh until tears came down their eyes. "I don't think you young'uns appreciate how serious this is!" he breathed in his fieriest pastor voice. Carl, seeing that Pastor Dellaroose was very upset, calmed himself before answering.

"Pastor that is one of the reasons we're here."

This seemed to take the pastor a moment to process before he slowly sat back on the couch.

"You mean you want to get married?" Shock or skepticism or both were heavy in his tone.

Lois chimed in respectfully. "Pastor, I'm not sure if 'want to' is accurate. Carl and I have discussed it and we both recognize that what the Lord wants is more important than our own ideas of how we would meet the person meant for us."

Pastor Dellaroose breathed a long sigh and whispered a "thank you", with his eyes lifted toward heaven, before refocusing on the couple before him.

"Well children, there is more. The purpose the Lord is laying out before you is going to be extremely dangerous." The Pastor looked as if he'd lost some of his height with this last statement. I was not told or shown if you would be successful."

Carl looked at Lois and then back to the pastor before his gaze came to rest on the twins. "Maybe, Always, would you be our witnesses?"

***

The ceremony was simple.

In a veil and dress borrowed from the twins, so long that Maybe and Always had to hold up both sides, Lois walked to the makeshift altar put up by volunteers. She held wild daisies from the nearby field in her hands.

Carl who stood waiting with Pastor Dellaroose thought she looked like a queen.

Lois trembled as she approached her husband to be. "Lord", she thought, "Please show me this is not a crazy mixed up decision." She lifted her eyes to find Carl staring at her. In his eyes she found the Lord's answer.

The ceremony was quick, but anointed and Maybe and Always sang "I Love You Truly" as Lois and Carl shared their first kiss after saying their "I do's". For Lois, the kiss was the most wonderful part of the ceremony. She was so nervous beforehand she thought she might throw up. What if he had bad breath? What if she was repelled by his kiss? Instead she found warmth, and preciousness, and home. It was instantaneous, and she knew Carl had felt it too.

She blushed prettily afterward, and Carl touched her face with his hand and smiled. Before much more could be shared between them, Pastor Dellaroose grabbed both their hands to get their attention.

"Children I'm afraid we haven't much time for celebration." He began pulling them both back toward the bus with Maybe and Always trying to keep up as they held up Lois' wedding train.

***

As Carl and Lois arranged themselves on the small couch, and the twins assumed their sentinel positions in their rocking chairs, Pastor Dellaroose emerged from his bedroom area with his arms full of heaps of pages from sources that seemed to range from daily newspapers to government documents marked "Confidential".

He bent over and let the pages spill onto a small table produced from the pastor's room as well. The first thing to catch Carl's eye was a confidential document from Roswell's Airfield. He picked it up and began to scan it as Lois reached for a newspaper article from her home town of Albuquerque. It was the story of her grandparent's home being burned down! As she read farther she let out a gasp. "This says my grandparent's home burned down because of a gas leak!"

Carl instinctively reached out his hand covering hers and squeezing. "Don't worry sweetheart, we'll get to the truth." As was becoming the norm, Lois was immediately reassured. She smiled at Carl. "You called me sweetheart." Her blush punctuated the statement.

Carl smiled back. "Can't a man call his wife sweetheart?"

Lois laughed out loud. "You called me wife." This time Carl laughed too and leaned in for his second kiss from his wife. Lois was not afraid or unsure anymore and kissed him right back in front of the pastor and the twins.

Maybe and Always smiled at each other over the couples love talk. Pastor Dellaroose however, was not so understanding.

"Children please!" He was quite excited. "We've got so much to do before you leave tonight."

Carl looked at Lois in surprise and her own expression mimicked his.

"Tonight?" Confusion showed on Carl and Lois' faces.

"Yes!" The pastor's reply was vehement. "In my dream, you had a very small window before things would go terribly wrong. He thrust his hand toward Carl releasing a piece of paper containing a list of eight names. "Look at this." None of the names were familiar to Carl except for one. It was his Captain's name and it was first on the list. He handed it to Lois for her to peruse while he turned back to the pastor.

"Why is my Captain's name on this list, and who are these other people?"

Pastor Dellaroose was shaking his head back and forth even as Carl asked the question. "I'm sorry Carl, I wasn't given any detail about why these people are on the list. Only that each of them must be contacted by both of you together in the next month."

This time Lois spoke up. "...but, but how?"

Pastor Dellaroose did not pause when he responded, "In person."   After this last statement the pastor turned his back to the group and appeared to be wrestling with some inner conflict before coming to a decision within himself with a forceful nod of his head. When he finally spoke it was not a surprise to any present when he said, "Let us pray." They all bowed their heads, but this time Carl drew his wife's hand in his.

After the pastor blessed the gathering, his intent gaze returned to the newlyweds. "In my dream"...he hesitated, swallowing loudly, "In my dream, if you two do not accomplish the task the Lord has set before you...the results will be cataclysmic!"

***

Carl and Lois walked toward the entrance of the hospital with the weight of the world on their shoulders. Who were they? Who were they that the Lord should notice them?

The car ride back to the hospital had been filled with silence. Lois, scared and confused, was replaying her life to this point, looking for clues. Carl was wondering how he was going to allow this lovely creature next to him, whom he was already head over heels for, to participate in a dangerous game that could mean death to them both.

As they approached the doors to the entrance of the hospital, Carl instinctively took Lois' hand. It was as if the weight that bent them over was suddenly lifted. They both sensed it immediately and looked at each other for confirmation. The Lord had given his first gift to the couple, a wedding gift; strength in the bond of matrimony.

The hospital was quiet, but there was definitely noise coming from the wing that housed Lois' family. It was Mama Angel! Lois pulled Carl along as she picked up her pace, and walk-ran-shuffled toward her Mama's room. What greeted them at the doorway was nothing short of miraculous. All three of the children that had accompanied them on the trip to the revival ran around screaming and shouting. Mama sat up in her bed, smiling and chatting with...PAPA!

Lois screamed his name as she ran forward and hugged her Papa Gus around the neck. He sat in a wheel chair next to Mama's bed holding her hand as they watched the children run around, shushing them when they got too out of hand. Fortunately the woman who had been in the next bed was gone. Lois decided not to ask what had happened to her.

Remembering she had something very important to share, Lois cleared her throat loudly. The children noticed first. Mama and Papa Gus' attention was drawn by their children's sudden silence. Carl, who had stood back and watched her reunion with her adopted father, came and stood beside her taking her hand.

"Papa, Mama, kids" she was suddenly shy and hesitant. Before she could finish, Carl wrapped his arm around Lois, and grinning from ear to ear shouted, "We're married!" Lois was just a little put out by his abrupt announcement, but she smiled knowing these were things she'd have to get used to. She was so busy reprimanding herself she almost missed the

"What!" "Are you serious!" and finally, "Oh Niña, congratulations!" Without quite realizing what was about to happen, Lois began to weep. This was a day she'd dreamed of; her wedding day with all her family present. She told everyone they were tears of joy, but in truth, in herself, she knew she mourned for having to let go of the fantasy she'd had since she was a little girl; yards of lace, flowers, bridesmaids, and little tea cakes.

Mama Angel looked at her knowingly, "Don't worry Niña, when you get home, we'll have a real wedding for you both!" Lois smiled as she wiped away her tears for the past, instead of mourning what would not be, she jumped on Mama's bed and allowed herself to be enfolded in her mother's arms.

Papa Gus, who showed no signs of injury from his stroke, astutely suggested that he buy Carl and the children a juice at the nurse's station. As they left the room, Mama Angel took Lois' face in her hands, "I can't believe my baby is all grown up!"

She sniffled loudly. "Sweetie, I need to have a talk with you. Are you prepared for your wedding night?" Her concern showed on her face and the one good eye that stared at her from the bandages.

Lois blushed her pretty blush and looked at her Mama. "Well, I really don't have the particulars, but I've lived on a farm for some time."

Mama laughed. "Pull that chair over here and sit down. I'm going to give you a crash course."

***

Carl stood next to Gus' wheelchair by the nurse's station sipping juice as his wife received instruction on a successful wedding night.

Gus held up his juice carton in salute and Carl tapped it with his own. "Congratulations! If you hurt her I'll kill you and bury you in the desert." It was said with such serene malice that Carl did a double take and looked Gus in the eye. The seriousness of his comment showed in the steel in his eyes, and Carl smiled back, knowing they were going to get along just fine.

***

The arrangements for transportation were made to get Lois' family safely home. After much arguing, Papa Gus determined he would drive his truck back behind the ambulance transporting Mama Angel. It was early evening when Lois hugged her Mama, Papa, and adopted siblings and said good-bye. There were tears from both sides as Carl and Lois waved them God's speed back home.

Chapter 18

When they were out of sight, Carl turned to his new bride and grabbing her shoulders kissed her gently, but passionately on the mouth. He pulled away and stared into her eyes. "We'd better get going Mrs. Wedner. I checked on my old captain and he's living in Texas now. We'll have to drive quite a way. I've got a hotel room on the way so we can stop for the night."

Lois smiled back at Carl as he spoke but her thoughts were convoluted and fearful. She felt her smile stretch to the breaking point. Carl, who was becoming very attuned to his new wife, sensed her fear. "What's wrong? What's the matter Lois?" His question, asked in the right tone of voice, seemed to open the floodgates.

"I…I guess…I guess I'm just not sure how I got here Carl, and at the same time I know exactly how I got here and the two seem to be colliding in me." Carl, who'd had his own taste of fear and uncertainty understood her distress and was about to reassure her when she spoke again.

"I am not used to someone making all the decisions Carl. I've had to do that for myself for some time now and it feels a little invasive…I'm just telling you because I don't want to fight on our wedding night." Lois enfolded his hand in hers as she spoke to soften the words.

Carl started to reply angrily, but took a breath. This was new to both of them. He needed to take his time. He needed to pray. "Give me wisdom Lord." he whispered under his breath before continuing.

"Lois, I was not trying to make all the decisions, I was trying to care for you. I'm sorry if it felt as if I was taking over. It's what I know how to do. Organize, plan, execute."

It was Lois' turn to stop and consider. She really had to start thinking a different way. She was so used to taking care of herself. If this was going to work both of them were going to have to give a little.

"You're right of course Carl. I wouldn't even know where to begin. Maybe when we get to the hotel we can spend some time getting to know each other a little better. Talking."

Carl was smiling as she spoke until the word 'talking'. That was not what he had envisioned for their wedding night. She was trying however, and he wouldn't let her down.

"Well, Mrs., we have about a four hour drive before we stop for the night. Let's start talking and not stop til we reach our destination." This said with his wicked grin.

Lois blushed and nodded her head.

***

The next morning Lois woke in Post, Texas to the smell of coffee and a deep feeling of satisfaction. Carl was whistling in the bathroom as he shaved, and for just a moment Lois let her mind replay the gift she'd received the night before. Never in all of her imaginings...she smiled and giggled and felt like Scarlett O'Hara the day after she and Rhett conceived their second child. Now she understood Scarlett's smile! She was a woman.

It had not been perfect, and at times it had been very awkward, but her husband...hee

hee…her husband had been patient and gentle and caring…and she couldn't wait until tonight!

"Oh Lois! You little tart!" Her own voice chastised her, but she silenced it as she stepped out of her side (her side, hee hee) of the bed. She had just pulled on the new robe that Carl had presented as a gift after he'd carried her over the threshold of the Honeymoon Suite at the Hotel Algerita, when Carl stepped into the room grinning from ear to ear.

"Good morning Mrs. Wedner.", he sang as he pulled her into his arms and began to dance her around the room.

Lois laughed and danced with him before he swooped in for a kiss that left her knees weak. When she opened her eyes she saw that the serious Carl was now back.

"I'm afraid darling that we've got a bit of a tight schedule. How much time will you need to get ready before breakfast?" Lois was already heading for the bathroom. "Just give me thirty minutes…." she sang as she closed the door.

Carl learned then, and knew until the time of his death that thirty minutes of Lois time meant exactly one hour.

***

Carl and Lois were fast becoming more than newlyweds, they were becoming a team. They'd worked together to write a list of things to do once they reached Lubbock, Texas where Carl's old Captain now lived. They parked on Main Street and Lois kissed Carl on the cheek before crossing the street to register them in a hotel for the night. Carl walked to the nearest public phone to call his Captain and see if they could get over to see him within the next few hours.

He waited anxiously as the phone rang on the other line.

"Hello" a croak.

"Cap!" "Cap it's me Wedner."

"Wedner?" the voice on the other end of the line sounded confused.

"Cap, it hasn't been that long. Hey, I just got married! I'm here with the missus and I wanted to bring her by to meet you, whatdya say?"

"Wedner! Is that you?! Hell yes you can come by. It'll be good to see you old friend. Hey, hey, can you bring me a bottle of Bourbon? I'm fresh out, and I'd love to drink to you and your new wife's health."

"Sure Cap, sure. I just need your address."

"My address? Uh, sure my address...just a minute just a minute...here it is...here...ahem...

Carl listened as his captain gave him the address committing it to memory. His Captain sure sounded different. Carl hadn't heard any of his Captain's usual confidence and strength. He sounded foggy and old. As Carl promised to see him soon and hung up the phone he worried what he...they...would find when they arrived. "It's in your hands Lord."

***

Carl and Lois knew immediately upon their arrival at his Captain's lodgings that something was wrong. They pulled slowly to the curb in front of a rundown apartment building in East Lubbock. Carl knew that his Captain had received a generous retirement. There was no reason for him to be living here. The couple shared a glance, before clasping hands and praying. "Lord let your light shine before us. Amen."

Carl exited the car and came around to Lois' side to open her door. He grasped his wife's hand in his and started for the front of the building. Alcohol, Marijuana, and the smell of something rotten permeated the air.

Carl's Captain lived on the first floor in a one bedroom apartment. As they stepped up to the door and knocked, a scream could be heard above them and then shouts and cursing. Carl's cop instincts kicked in and he was just about to go investigate when Cap opened the door.

Carl was so shocked by what greeted them that he couldn't of helped Lois if her hair was on fire! His Captain, Captain J.L. Morgan, one of the toughest men Carl had ever met stood before them an emaciated and lost man. His eyes were watery and unfocused. His nose had grown to the size of a small lime with broken red veins running through it like a roadmap. He was missing one of his front teeth and his clothes hung on him like the imprisoned Jews they'd seen overseas.

Carl was so shocked that for a moment he thought, "we have the wrong place." But then his Captain smiled and Carl recognized a small piece of his friend was still there.

"Carl, you old turd, went and got yourself married did ya!?" His breath created a haze around his words and both Carl and Lois were knocked back by the strong odor of alcohol, before Cap stepped back waving and inviting them to "Come in, come in." Carl pushed Lois forward and watched as she stepped gingerly into the hovel that was the Cap's home.

"Sorry for the mess" and "Let's go out on the patio" were heard behind them as they entered. As the group walked toward the patio doors, they passed by piles and piles of reports marked confidential, most stained with food or pest droppings. They reached the patio and found it relatively clean except for some scattered bourbon bottles. Cap pointed Carl and Lois to a bench while he took the folding chair that sat by the door.

As soon as everyone found their seat, Carl jumped in, "Cap, I'd like you to meet my missus, Lois." Carl was beaming with pride as he said it and Cap looked at her quizzically and stuck out his hand.

"Pleasure to meet you Mrs. Wedner." His smile gave Lois a glance at his former charm. His next comment was aimed at her husband "Carl, "You ol' dog!" She looks too pretty for you!" They all laughed and then no one spoke for a few minutes.

Lois finding herself uncomfortable asked, "So...Mr. Morg...

Cap interrupted immediately, "Just call me Cap honey."

Lois looked at Carl to see if he was offended by this familiarity, but he just nodded at her, so she turned back and started again. "So, Cap, how long have you lived in Lubbock?"

Before the Cap answered he turned to Carl. "Hey buddy, you bring that bourbon?" Carl was a little surprised. Cap had been no stranger to a drink now and then, but he was obviously a slave to it now.

"Ya, sure Cap." "I'll go pour you one while you and Lois talk."

Cap turned back to Lois. "Well, little lady", he began, "I've been here for about a year now."

He paused as Carl returned with his drink. He took it and saluted Carl with the glass, which

Carl automatically returned, making Lois giggle. Cap took a large swallow of bourbon before continuing "Yea, yea about a year now." He looked Carl in the eye for a moment. "I left a year to the day after we were out at the ranch. You know what I'm talking about Carl." It was a statement.

Carl replied anyway. "Yes Cap, I remember."

"Well", Cap continued, "It seems that we were all wrong...all wrong..." he began to fade visibly. Tears filled his eyes and he hung his head, mumbling. Carl and Lois shared worried looks over his head. They both understood almost at the same moment that the incident Carl had been involved in was tied by divine strings to Lois' own experience with her grandparents' farm. Now they needed to find out how, but Cap seemed in no condition at the moment to help them.

Lois grabbed Carl's hand and bent her head. She had learned her lesson to this point. Carl quickly followed her lead. He grabbed his Cap's hand and bowed his head.

"Lord, reveal your design and intent. Help my Cap. Bring him clarity. Amen."

Cap seemed to realize that they were praying, and shook his hand violently free. "What the hell....what is this crap!" Carl was so stunned by his response that he did not reply, but Lois did.

"Cap, we've been sent here on a mission. We need to know what's happened. We need to know why you left a year to the day. It will save many lives." Carl sat in awe as his wife cleverly played to his captain's sense of duty. He jumped in while they had the offensive.

"That's right Cap. We've been sent to you on a mission. Can you help us or not?"

Cap seemed to sit up just a little straighter. His eyes cleared…just a bit. Through his foggy mind ran thoughts of former glories when he'd been brave and strong and true. "Of course I can help you!" he said over loud. "What's the mission?" Carl leaned over and kissed his brilliant wife before continuing.

"Cap, I need you to talk to me about the beings we saw. You told me back at the site where we found them that they were going to make us gods. Could you start by explaining that?"

Carl would never forget the words that followed. His Captain began to relate a story that left Carl and Lois believing theirs was a suicide mission.

Area 51 Outside Nevada, 1948

It had been just over a year since the crash landing of two space ships outside Roswell, New Mexico. Dr. John Felner had been assigned as a corpsman the day they brought the guests to his duty station. He worked hand in hand with Captain J.L Morgan who was one of only a few survivors from the initial discovery of the craft.

From all of the data being received, almost two hundred men who'd accompanied the General that fateful night, had died of a wasting sickness within eight months of being exposed to the crash site. Mitigation to stop the contagion once it was identified had been difficult.

In the end all that could be done was to bring them to the underground bunker and make them comfortable while they died. The beings that brought the sickness had also come to stay.

Dr. Felner found it was uncomfortable spending time with the beings. Their language skills made it difficult communicate. Most times all that came from them were impressions...pictures really, that explained little. These impressions were always accompanied by a low buzzing noise, like people talking in the background.

Captain Morgan, who followed the beings around taking extensive notes seemed to understand their needs, and believed whole-heartedly that these beings were a master race that had come to bring the United States of America universal knowledge. The being who seemed to be in charge, Random, had explained in its picturesque way, that Chaos, Randomness, and Confusion were what ordered the universe. It was odd, Dr. Felner thought, how often the beings spoke in threes.

The being explained at length that their names, like spoken language, had little or nothing to do with truth and so were unimportant. While humans had decided that language would dictate the world's maturity, Random explained, words, languages, and communication were in fact small blips in evolutionary cycles. Technology, it was emphasized graphically, combined with human biology, would be what led to the stabilization of earthly kingdoms.

Random guaranteed that within one hundred years, if humans would allow he and his fellow travelers to, layer by layer subscribe a new world order, a transcendental peace accompanied by complete universal knowledge for all humankind would be achieved. The movers and shakers of the United States were intrigued and very excited about being the world government that brought this enlightenment, but they were to be disappointed in this endeavor.

Random made it quite clear that their ships were not the first to arrive. It was explained, again in pictures of eras gone by, how their race had been endeavoring to bring about this new world order for several millennia. Much to the chagrin of the powers that be, it was explained that Adolph Hitler had been the closest human yet to reach the critical mass needed to bring about the changes they described, but the beings also gave examples of ancient civilizations such as the Medo-Persians, and Babylonians.

When questioned about these leaders who were considered evil, vile men, Random explained that most of these great men had each achieved partial success because they'd been genetically engineered by Random's species. They had been nurtured through carefully planned abductions, had been given very specific instructions, and for all intents and purposes, been given the ability to accomplish it…but, (and here Random became enraged) failure continued. All of this, of course, Random assured, was because the technological advances of humankind had been so slow to develop that its' race, in a gesture of celestial brotherhood, had tried to speed it along.

"Why look at the Atom bomb", it persuaded, its initial destruction was horrific, but hadn't it also assured peace in the world for decades to come?" He encouraged those present to stop looking at everything linearly. Some things had to be; to cycle newness into human existence.

"The discovery of nuclear energy", Random persuaded, "also allowed their species to 'pierce the veil' or hyper-jump into their dimension more effectively.   The destructive force of nuclear energy was helpful, but there was, the being stated, "a creative force" in the atom as well. This force, It promised, would be one of the instruments the beings used to help humanity achieve eternal life.

Chapter 19

Random let the information he'd shared thus far sync. This was the important part, which had always been a pivotal point in trying to create their Master's race.

It would begin with six viruses.

As the usual protests began regarding viruses and the American people, Random spoke pictorially of the virus as a conduit, showing the group that at the cellular level, a virus was one of the best ways to spread good as well as bad. Those in the room were so overwhelmed with what they'd just been shown, they were speechless.

The scientists in the room wanted to run to their labs and begin experimenting immediately with this astounding revelation, but Random stopped them by holding up a thin arm in its now familiar imitation of a 'hail Hitler'. Now that they'd seen a small bit of truth, Random felt they were adequately prepared to hear the lie. It took so little really. Random politely requested that each of them, armed with this new knowledge, open themselves to a truth that would be foreign to all they'd known before. These viruses were going to rapidly bring the United States to a point of readiness for the new world order that was equal to their European and Asian counterparts

According to the beings, in order to create a master race capable of eternal life, humans must be vaccinated from the relative term of "sin". This could of course be accomplished, he went on to relay, through a lengthy inoculation period which would assist the humans in building immunity to subtle DNA changes. These changes would reduce the noise created by a "guilty conscience" if you will. After the initial outline of how the viruses worked, Random explained what each of them was and how they would shape the collective masses.

Adultery/fornication was first, and probably the most shocking, once the purpose for the viruses was disclosed.   Sin, the visitor explained, was an evolutionary idea that allowed the sustainability of human life. Without parameters, in the days when the missing link actually stood upright, man would have remained a chimp killing or being killed.

As thought and reason began to seep into the new homogenous species, the visitor continued, it became readily apparent that boundaries were needed to sustain the species.   These boundaries, Random noted, were now antiquated and were keeping the dominant species of the planet from achieving their next evolutionary step…immortality.

Marriage and family were still a cultural tradition that kept humans imprisoned in a biased stasis. It must be the first broken for the other viruses to be effective.   The virus spreading from person to person with only approximately one hundred thousand beings infected, would achieve maximum saturation in approximately ten to fifteen years.

Random explained that the viruses spoken of would change humankind intrinsically in the construction of their cells, literally redefining or as Random put it "rewriting the human DNA script." Adultery/fornication would also help with the absorption rate of the other six viruses, which took longer to reach saturation. In other words, the first virus would create a snowball effect on the absorption rates of the other viruses.

As the being began to discuss the other five viruses and their mechanics, most of the human heads in the room could be seen bobbing up and down, but Dr. Felner looked stricken. This being was talking about deadly sins. Dr. Felner was also an Army Rabbi. His own feelings of disgust and fear at what the Random was suggesting made him speak up.

"So, you are saying that in order for us to achieve immortality, we must become immoral?"

There was no mistaking the hatred and malice directed at him by the Random. Nausea and a sense of vertigo made Dr. Felner wobble and topple to the floor.

Random turned to Captain Morgan who had been busily transcribing and recording the conversation. "Kill him." Random ordered.

The being could not have been clearer, but Captain Morgan hesitated. Americans didn't kill each other, they killed the enemy. The captain's conscious-self felt heat like a red hot poker sear off any part of him that connected his decency his moral fortitude to his soul. He pulled out his gun and shot Dr. Felner in the head.

The initial reaction of those gathered in the room was shock and fear. No one moved. As Dr. Felner lay on the linoleum floor of the conference room, the blood from the fatal gunshot wound pooling around him on the floor, "they were" Carl's Cap explained, "frozen in a moment of decision, one of those moments in time where histories were forged."

Captain Morgan's voice shrank to a whisper as he confided how he'd felt in that moment; strong, powerful, invincible! He was he shared, becoming immortal.

After several ticks on the room's clock, guards appeared and removed the body, signaling the decision of those present. Random focused again on the audience.

"We must have order and complete agreement. Our species does not want to overrun and control your world, neither do we want dissension. It was, Random chastised, the downfall of all of their previous efforts, generally by the Jews and/or Christians who had so enmeshed themselves in religious practices that their continued interference was hindering the whole of humanity."

After this last communication, the Random sat expressionless, as the orderlies cleaned the blood from the floor next to its seat, before continuing with 'the plan'.

"The first virus", he continued a bit agitated by the interruption, "would spark several societal changes." By the time of saturation of the first virus, estimated to be approximately 1962, offspring of the generation would begin to rebel against current government standards.

The generation would also provide a window to self-discovery, equality for women, and freedom from cultural biases against other races (*a little lie to create the illusion of evolving*).

At the height of this counter-revolution, the next virus would be released. Here the being paused, as was noted by the slack-jaws and staring eyes of the humans in attendance.

Imbeciles! Idiots! Morons! This is what they were thrown over for? This pathetic race of naïve sniveling primordial dust!? Random allowed himself just a few moments of rage before he continued.   Focus was required. Crowns and domination were imminent.

He recaptured the attention of the group and continued. "The next virus to be released would be Greed. Now here, this would be a fun one." and the group sensed a note of glee in the telling.

Greed was the next evolutionary virus. The accumulation of things, at any price, would create the first tier or level of humans to be considered for the Master race.   Those just willing to trudge along doing menial work for twenty to forty years, with no recognition or attention would become the slaves of those willing to put in every effort to get what they desired. Envy, he explained was like a booster shot that would help achieve critical mass and would be given at the same time. The saturation point   for   the   virus   and   its booster...approximately ten years after its introduction. This would take them close to 1980, when greed would reach critical mass.

Since Random had silenced the dissenting voice, no one in the room dared to share any additional concerns. Each of them understood that the beings had the power to communicate their thoughts and suggestions upon the group; they also understood that the beings had no telepathic capabilities to actually 'read' their minds.

Random   however,   was   completely unconcerned about what was on their minds.

The Vine was returning to Israel. The stage was set. This small piece of dirt, and all the insects living on it, would rot in hell.

As the Random pictographed images of the changes each successive virus would ignite as it was released, each person's head was filled with machinery and technologies they'd only dreamed about.

The next virus was Random's least favorite. This was relayed with pictures of millions of grotesquely fat humans lying in bed and eating, eating, eating.

"Gluttony", said the being, "will weed out those with little or no self-control." This particular virus will also be helped along as food shortages begin and new, genetically altered foods begin to transform human DNA. This will cause innumerous health issues, but will also spawn new medical advances in sequencing the creation key.

Random switched the pictographs playing in his audience's head, providing pictures of mutations of food that allowed nourishment to fifty people instead of five all while tasting great!   This virus would only take five years to reach saturation.

Next, was…oh how to put it…next was addiction.   The Random explained in some detail that this would be the easiest. Since the release of the four previous viruses, humankind will have taken to using alcohol and other drugs to stem the uncomfortable feelings generated from the changes the viruses have on the human psyche.

Concurrently, the Random shared, new pharmacological advances will allow the countries leaders to produce formularies that lulled the moral center of the brain into passivity; all while instilling in the masses that pain was not necessary when such medicines were available. "This was necessary" Random stated, "before revolution could occur. (A picture of a Russian flag and a Vodka bottle were used for illustration)." The virus would only take three and one half years to reach maturation.

The next two were always the most difficult and uncomfortable; Anger and Cruelty. Random glanced around the room. It could see the captive audience would not have trouble with these last two, but they were no decision makers.

Pausing, the Random provided a request to Captain Morgan to bring his General and any persons of state that were available into the room before he would continue…another pause and Captain Morgan alone was given a name. Like a prophet of old Captain Morgan spoke it aloud, "Bring in Stewart Bohner."

Several minutes later, a retinue of military personnel and talking heads entered. Random knew they'd been watching through the double-sided glass window in the room. Knew that they were aware of the plan thus far, and knew they wanted to hear the rest.

Bohner was a man known to them all. An eccentric multi-millionaire said to worship blasphemies as a high ranking Mason or Illuminati. To a man they could relate stories of perversities barely able to be thought of much less spoken out loud. Disgusting, unnatural, and excessive, women were said to bring their children to him to be used and…some whispered…sacrificed, though no charges had ever been brought against him. Most had scoffed at the conspiracy theories surrounding him, but sitting her now, they began to see and believe.

A break was taken and red phones were dialed. Within an hour Stewart Bohner appeared behind the dark glass. As his eyes focused on the being sitting in the enclosed room before him, tears welled in his eyes.   High ranking officials watched in astonishment as this powerful man opened the door stood before Random, and then fell to his knees in obeisance.

The lesser in the room were excused, except for Captain Morgan, whose worship and adoration appeared to appease the pride of the enlightened being in their midst.

Everyone found a seat except Bohner who stayed at Random's feet like a pet, as the being continued lightly stroking his new acolyte's head. "Anger, yes anger….would be largely boosted by the previous viral releases, and was necessary to continue the break-down of traditional values most particularly in the family unit setting.

Individuality, self-esteem, and personal growth could not be achieved when tied to the emotions of a set of people sharing the same bloodline.   Self-actualization, self-awareness, and self-preservation were all uniquely tied to one's ability to self-evolve to their highest potential.

This was not achievable, unfortunately, without causing a breakdown of the norms of current societal practices on planet earth.

Anger and Cruelty would increase 'crime' per se, but would also weed out the weak, and provide soldiers in the army of the new world order.   With no familial ties, humans as a species would find ways to congregate together, would find things to be righteously angry about together, and would come together to join the world population rather than continuing to babble patriotic dribble.

Using these viruses, the Random concluded, and strategic social engineering, the United States would finally join its brothers and sisters in uniting under a new centrally ruled world government.   This final staging, which would occur after many of those in the room were dead, would allow the "Singularity" or Event of immortality to occur.

Random watched the inferiors, entertained. The beginning of the 'coming' was underway.

As they bent their heads to scribble on pads of paper, or make phone calls on the red phone, and argued about roles and responsibilities, he quietly released the most critical virus into the room...the one that came from the cellular construction of its own dermas...Pride.

Captain J.L. Morgan's Apartment, Lubbock, TX 1950

Cap sat back and looked blearily at his guests. He could feel the pull of the power surge from reliving the event.   He knew that although his body was sick, the salvation he'd been guaranteed was on its way.   Hadn't Random told him so when he'd began to sicken? Carl, his old buddy was looking perplexed.   He obviously didn't recognize the immortality that rested inside his new improved Cap.

Carl watched as Cap reached for another swig from his bourbon. His hand shook as he took it.

"Cap", he started unsure how to process what he'd just heard. He looked to Lois for guidance. They were both so overwhelmed by what they'd just heard, questions dogpiled in their thoughts, making it difficult to determine where to begin.

Lois squeezed his hand and smiled. "Cap, why did you leave?"

Cap took another pull on his Bourbon before answering calmly, "Oh it's this damn wasting sickness." As he said it he began to cough. It wracked his body, and his lungs sounded as if they'd deflate any minute. He sucked in air like it was his bourbon before slumping back in his chair. His smile was grim, and a small dot of blood appeared at the corner of his mouth. Before Carl could comment on it, Cap wiped his mouth with the back of his hand, and continued speaking.

"Almost everyone involved got the wasting sickness", he wheezed. "It's because of the power of these beings Carl! They are gods. Just being in their presence causes our human forms to wither away. Everything inside us just turns to mush." Cap's countenance had transformed to maniacal gleam.

Carl looked at Lois once again, who in her straightforward fashion shrugged her shoulders. He turned back to Cap.

"Cap, I don't understand." He said quietly looking his old captain in the eye, "If these beings are going to make us immortal, why does everyone they're around die?"

Cap, who'd managed to recover from his coughing bout, grabbed his bourbon bottle by the neck and hugged it to his chest. "Because my boy", he stated emphatically saluting the unseen, "only the strong will survive!"

Chapter 20

Lois and Carl sat in their car in shock, staring out the window quietly while their hands met in the middle of the seat. Where to begin? What does one even say to an alien race taking over the earth? Were these really extraterrestrials? Were they demons? All of these questions raced back and forth between them, but neither knew how to begin to discuss it. The silence was finally broken when Carl cleared his throat and asked, "What's the next name on our list?"

Lois who'd been 'praying/thinking' jumped just a little at the sound of her husband's voice. She mumbled a bit while reaching into her handbag to find the list Pastor Dellaroose had given them for their trip. Pulling it out, Lois unfolded it and handed it to Carl.

"Reverend Larry (Bubba) Hart." Both of them stared at the name as it had been neatly typed by Maybe, and began to giggle. Quietly at first, trying very hard to conceal it, and then giving in as each of them practiced the name Bubba over and over again. The knowledge they were both on the edge of hysteria floated above them like a mist. Had the Lord made them responsible for saving the world from these aliens / demon beings? It seemed such a stretch for two small town country folk. Carl reached over and kissed Lois on the mouth. As he drew away he suggested a prayer before they went to see Bubba.

***

Reverend Larry 'Bubba' Hart lived in Dallas Texas in a downtown pay-by-the-day hotel room. He'd moved into the hotel after his wife had left him.   Apparently he nurtured his drinking habit instead of her.

Five years later, he'd mostly succeeded in giving up the booze. The Lord had found him in a bar spending his last dollar on a poor man's scotch and soda.   He'd been contemplating drinking himself to death if he could panhandle enough to see the job done. It had been his low, his rock bottom if you will.

At that precise moment, a preacher named Pastor Dellaroose and his two cousins had walked into the bar, shouted for him by name, and commanded him to "Come outside a moment please."

Bubba, surprised and a little annoyed to be interrupted had sidled off his barstool, walked out into the light, and never looked back.

The Lord had been searching for Bubba and he knew it, but Bubba was angry about the losses that had shrunk his life. Stubbornness and pain had tuned out the calling, so God sent reinforcements in the form of the pastor and his cousins. He'd fallen to his knees right there on the sidewalk outside the bar and relinquished control of his life to his Lord and Savior once again.

Now he mostly stayed in his room, rummaging through stacks and stacks of newspapers, magazines, science fiction stories and supernatural phenomena periodicals.   Almost from the beginning, the Lord had shown him things in the world he would have rather not known.

The walls of his room had become papered with significant articles of information all tied together with green string leading from one article to the next. To an unknowing eye it was madness…it was lunacy…it was zealotry!

Fortunately for Bubba, he didn't mind being a zealot. It fit the rightness in him to focus intently on words, events, and cause and effect. He had used these skill sets, before the drink had taken all his attention, to keep a record of Satan's movements toward a new world order.

Today he scratched out a living preaching on street corners with a hat in his hand. He always had enough. The Lord always provided. So he was not particularly surprised when he received a call from Mr. and Mrs. Wedner saying that "Pastor Dellaroose had given them his name and they wanted to come by for a visit if that was possible."

Bubba was trying to straighten his small living space when the knock came on the door. He straightened and spoke out loud "I know Lord, I know, I'll take it easy on them." before moving to the door to open it for his guests.

***

Carl and Lois stood in the doorway of Reverend Hart's small apartment a little dumbstruck.

This was the second person on their list who'd cracked their preconceived mold of important people to meet. Reverend Hart filled the doorway so that his head was not even visible as they both stood with their neck's craned back trying to look up to see his face

Bubba bent his head and let out a "boo!" in a baritone that breached the hallways. Lois jumped, but Carl who'd been taught in the service to reach past his fear stuck out his hand and replied, "Reverend Bubba I presume?"

The statement/question was a direct hit to the Reverend's funny bone and he began to laugh a rich booming laugh. He wiped the tears of laughter from his eyes while he grabbed Carl's hand to shake it. Carl's eyes grew just a little wider as his hand was enveloped in what should have been a catcher's mitt.

"Come in, come in", the Reverend invited, stepping aside to allow room for them to pass.

"Reverend Hart, I'd like to introduce my wife Lois, and I'm Carl. I believe Pastor Dellaroose told you to expect us…" The Reverend was already shaking his head yes as he interrupted, "Yes Dellaroose called, please come in and sit down."

Lois, who'd stepped into the apartment and moved to the side as the men spoke, looked around the room they'd entered. What she saw terrified her. There was no space on the walls, or ceiling for that matter, not littered with paper. As she continued her perusal of the room she followed the green strings connecting all the articles to the center of the ceiling.

What she saw there made her gasp in horror. It was a picture of her grandparents' farm. It was the front page article that had appeared in the local newspaper explaining the tragedy. Her gasp caused both men to halt their conversation and stare at her. She didn't notice at first, so intent was her gaze on the ceiling.

With a slight polite cough, Carl stepped over to his wife and touched her shoulder. "Are you all right honey?" he asked with concern. Lois slowly drew her gaze away, turned toward her husband, pointed her finger upward and uttered one word, "Look!"

Both the Reverend and Carl looked upward to where Lois pointed. Carl's eyes widened, but Reverend Hart's became fiery with righteous indignation. The Fallen Ones.

"Reverend", Lois began.

"Please, I'd feel more comfortable if you both just called me Bubba."

Lois nodded and continued, "Bubba, that is…was…my grandparent's home."

"Ahhh", Bubba exhaled deeply, "why don't we all sit down and I will try and explain what you're looking at." Carl took Lois by the arm and led her over to the two small wobbly chairs Bubba had pulled close to what appeared to be his armchair/bed.

He turned to the Reverend and suggested, "Why don't we tell you what we know first Bubba so you know what information we've gathered so far." Bubba liked Carl; Straight forward, to the point, and intelligent.

Yes the Lord had sent these people and the time was at hand, even at the door…he giggled out loud at his own wit, which was completely incongruous with his size, then apologized to his visitors. "I'm not used to company as you can imagine. Bubba took his seat and asked Carl to fill him in.

Outside of Time

Beginnings.

Beginnings could be as helpful as endings; or as tragic. The farm. That dust spot existing on the Master's property; the destruction had been an unplanned Random event! The breach widened like a uterine contraction allowing Random, along with a small contingency, to break through.

As the Vine returns, the veil stretches thinner and thinner like the cervix of the Great Whore of Babylon as she labors. Breaking the barrier, piercing the veil, had been better than the Random rape of a virgin girl. Constructing the Random act of the death of these three was a gift, another little gem for the treasure box.

***

Carl started at the beginning, trying very hard to leave nothing out.

Sitting in this cramped hotel room, filled with such startling and horrific details, he understood a little better, the bond being created between his new wife and himself. They worked in tandem like a well-oiled machine. He and Bubba would discuss their mission and she would listen and interrupt every so often with bits of information they had not considered.

When he finished his explanation, Carl turned to his wife with a question in his eyes…had he left anything out? Lois gave a quick shake of her head letting him know they'd shared all they could. They both looked back to Bubba. They were startled to find he had fallen asleep; at least he looked as if he'd fallen asleep in his chair.

His eyes were closed, his head was back and his breathing was even.

"Um"…Carl began, before both he and Lois were thrown back in their chairs when Bubba jumped up and began doing what could only be described as an Irish jig.

Bubba turned circles around his small cramped room, laughing at times, crying at others, before he finally returned to his seat wiping his eyes and smiling at the both of them.

"I know you must think I'm crazy", he put up a hand so they would not protest (although the couple had no plan to do so).

"I must admit", he continued, "There have been plenty of times when I was sure of it!" He laughed again before saying more, before his voice choked with emotion. "But", he sputtered tears now forming again at the corner of his eyes, "Our God is a loving God, He will not suffer us to see corruption!"

He looked around his room again, making a broad sweeping motion with his large arm that encompassed the crazy maze of string and paper. "I thought this was all for me, so I would know and could preach His word, but I was wrong and I'm so grateful for it!"

His next comment was so matter of fact after his dance performance that it had Lois and Carl babbling as if they were speaking in tongues. "So", he wanted to know, "when do we leave?"

NE Wedner Farm, 2001

Lois sat back; scattered around her lay old photos, maps, papers…her life really. She looked up at the family before her and the realization that their adventure was just beginning struck her dumb. Full circle, that's where they'd come and now here she sat ready to become the Beloved's "Bubba".

Sara picked up a picture showing a very handsome man with his arm proudly around a beautiful young woman. They were both smiling as they stood in front of a circus tent. "Is this you and Carl", she asked as she handed the picture to her friend.

Lois took the picture from her hands and stared at it. "Was she really ever that young…?"

"Yes that's my Carl" she sighed heavily. Bubba's actually taking the picture. He came with us back to see Pastor Dellaroose and the twins before our journey really began."

Lois pondered how to continue the story and get the Beloved family moving, when a notebook, carelessly tossed in the life debris on the floor, caught her eye. She picked it up, and looking at her guests, decided that Annie should be the one to reveal what came next. She extended her hand and the book towards her. Annie's eyes opened wide in surprise. "Oh no Lois, I couldn't possibly read your personal journals", she protested. Lois as usual was having none of it.

***

"Annie, I've found on my journey that no matter what, no matter how, no matter when, God remains the same. If I remember correctly from our dinner conversations, you are the keeper of your family journals. There is always one who chronicles." She pressed the journal into Annie's hand. "Now, where was I…oh yes…turn to October tenth, nineteen hundred and seventy-six."

Annie's face was a question mark of embarrassment, but she bent her head and opened the leather-bound journal. She scanned through it quickly, not paying attention to anything but the dates. She needn't have worried.

The date which Lois had requested stood out on the page, not because of a star or ribbon marking the spot, but because it was crinkled and brittle, as if it had gotten wet. Lois nodded encouragement as Annie began to read.

October 10, 1976 Chanute, KS – Jim Igot Farm

...Subject is prostrate on the floor and has not eaten for eight days...Continued profanity and obscene gestures in response to our presence... Carl has been a champion. Bubba seems to be struggling, which is unusual. I fear the boy may be killed.

The first of the viruses is reaching saturation. Psychic activity, Satanism, and demon possession are so overwhelming, that I fear we are pushing against the tide (here more words but smudged and illegible, as if tears had spilt on the pages).

This little boy, this precious little boy, with his beautiful angelic face, blond hair, and small frame, has been tortured for days. If the Lord does not intervene and exercise this demon soon, he'll die!

Bubba is beside him praying...WHAT IS THAT!

Wedner Farm 2001

Annie looked up. "That's it.", she said quietly. The room and its occupants sat motionless.

Sara, who was going crazy with curiosity, finally blurted, "What happened?"

Lois had been crying silently as Annie read. It had been a horrific and terrifying day. The worst day of her life, truth be told. Worse even than when Carl went home to be with the Lord, and Lois expressed that to the Beloved's sitting quietly all around her.

Sara, without a thought reached over and laid her hand on Lois' shoulder, squeezing gently to encourage Lois to continue. Lois patted the hand on her shoulder and looked at each of the Beloveds. It had to be told. It had to be.

She began to quietly relate the story, but her voice grew in strength as she continued. "It was the Random", she explained. "It had been so long since we'd seen any of the beings…over twenty years… we were caught completely off guard."

***

October 10, 1976 Chanute, KS – Jim Igot Farm

Lois jumped to her feet as a shimmering of the air and crackling of lightning began to create pressure in the large barn they were working in. "What is that!" she screamed, but her voice was sucked out by the vacuum that had been created in an instant.

Bubba, lumbering to his feet beside the boy, was caught off guard when his oxygen was cut off by the thin arms of the boy around his throat. In a split second, he had curled his body around Bubba's back like a spider and was biting him on the neck and shoulders.

In between biting the boy would lift his head, stare at Carl and Lois, and scream in an unearthly voice, "You're next you pig, you sow, you're next!" Bubba struggled mightily to remove the arms tightening like a vise on his windpipe, but they would not budge. He was beginning to lose consciousness when the Random appeared through the shimmering.

The boy popped off Bubba's back like a tic and scrabbled over to the Random's side, kneeling next to him like a dog. Random reached down and petted the boy's head, which the boy responded to by panting heavily. Bubba, who'd begun to regain consciousness on the floor where he'd fallen in a heap, began making grunting noises.

"He's infected, he's infected", the little boy screeched in a sing song voice.

Carl, who'd rushed to Lois' side as soon as the shimmering began, was reciting the Lord's Prayer. He grabbed Lois' hand and they both raced to Bubba's side. Before they reached him however, the little spider boy jumped thirty feet in the air landing at the feet of Bubba's body curled up on the floor. The boy stood tall. He exuded anger and hatred. He spoke in his father's voice. "Say good-night Stevie." This was made all the more abhorrent because the group assembled to help him had been told that Steve had been raped repeatedly by his step-father who would always make him say those words after he had abused him.

Without pausing, the boy wrapped his arms around Bubba's head once again, and as Bubba began to pray for deliverance Steve, a broken little boy, snapped his neck.

Outraged, and horrified, Carl and Lois stopped in their rush to Bubba's side and screamed out their pain. Then like whispered refreshment, they remembered all Bubba had taught them and kneeling, began to speak The Word. The spirit descended on them and tongues of flames ignited on their foreheads. They began to speak to the Random and the minion residing in little Steve.

They spoke in an ancient language that neither understood, but the demons apparently did and their wails of anger and frustration began to pierce the eardrums of the couple. Both bent under the pain of the vile creatures outpouring of diseased vitriol, but continued to let the spirit of the Lord fight the battle. The pressure in the room became unbearable, and just when they believed that this was the end of the journey for them as well, another being appeared in the room.

Brilliant and white with a wing-span that seemed to fill the room, this being filled the Wedners and the room with hope! A sword of solid gold in the angel's hand (for Lois knew from her own experience it was indeed an angel) was held high and flashed and glimmered as it was directed toward the Random. Its bright countenance uncovered the dark in every corner, and the angel uttered only three words... "Lord rebuke you!"

With a final cry of outrage, the Random shimmered and began to disappear, when a flash from the angel's sword touched the top of little Steve's head and a black swarm of flies rose from him like a vapor. It and Random were sucked into the shimmering, and disappeared.

***

The room was silent, like a pause between breaths in a solemn conversation. Carl and Lois on their knees looked up and around. The angel now stood over Bubba's still form. Carl and Lois heartbroken, frightened, and lost, walked in reverence over to where the angel stood next to Bubba lifeless body.

The angel turned to them and said in a voice majestic with love, "Praise our Lord son of man, praise our Lord daughter of man, a warrior sits with our Lord tonight."

They worshipped the God of the universe through their sorrow. It was beautiful and heartbreaking, neither of them aware of time or how long they stood there. Their mourning ended abruptly, when they heard the coughing. Carl and Lois in their grief had forgotten about the little boy. Rushing over they laid their hands on him and began to pray. When they looked back, the angel was gone.

NE 2001, Wedner Farm

Lois dried her eyes with an embroidered handkerchief and rubbed her hand over a picture she'd found of Bubba standing next to the Bannister twins.

She laughed out loud at the private memory of Maybe and Always fighting for his attention. She looked up and was humbled to find that each of the Beloved's cried with her. "There was no time for this, they needed to get moving." She stood to her feet, brushing away her grief with the dust on her pants.

"You all need to be aware of what we're up against here. The danger has only increased over time. As the veil thins between our dimensions, Satan becomes bolder in his attacks. He knows his time is short."

She turned and started for an old leather suitcase wedged in a pile of junk at the back of the attic. She paused when she heard John Beloved ask the room in general, "We're up against?"

Without turning around, Lois answered the question each of them was thinking. "Yes

Beloved family, I'm your Bubba, and I'm coming with you!"

Before a word either in the negative or affirmative could be spoken, Lois raised her finger to her lips. Each Beloved closed their mouths respectfully. "I've received a list" Her voice was a whisper, "It is the beginning of your purpose Beloved family, and I've been given permission to travel with you."

She carried the suitcase toward the stairs but turned back, her face a roadmap of understanding. "You must each agree to accept this purpose, or the Lord will reach out to those ready to accept their destiny."   The Beloveds, who still sat on the floor in a circle, looked at each other and then inwardly into their hearts. Almost as one, a slight nod. Lois' smile lit up the attic. "Let's pray and thank the Lord for this opportunity to serve, and then we have to get on the road, John would you lead us?"

As they bowed their heads, a flame ignited on each forehead and as they stood to praise the name of the one true God, four new warriors joined the army of the Lord.

The End.

www.ingramcontent.com/pod-product-compliance
Lightning Source LLC
Chambersburg PA
CBHW061143040426
42445CB00013B/1519